Understand Derivatives in a Day

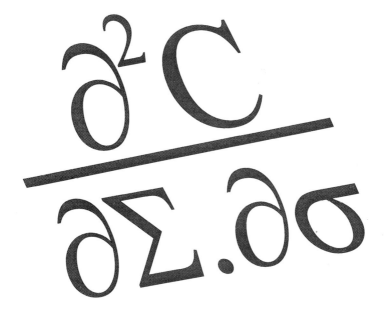

$$\frac{\partial^2 C}{\partial \Sigma . \partial \sigma}$$

Stefan Bernstein

D1104651

TTL is an imprint of
Take That Ltd.
P.O.Box 200,
Harrogate
HG1 2YR
ENGLAND

email:sales@takethat.co.uk

www.takethat.co.uk

**You should take independent financial advice before
acting on material contained in this book.**

TTL are always keen to receive ideas and manuscripts for new financial books.
Please send details to the address above.

ISBN 1-873668-92-9

Contents

4

Acknowledgements

I would like to thank all those fund managers and investment professionals who gave so freely of their time in helping to make this subject accessible to the ordinary investor, and those organisations which retain me to keep a guiding hand on their own trading strategies.

I also thank Pieski whose management of the Bernstein household during the often stressful production of this work was invaluable.

Without Madelaine England, Zeppi Kodenberg, Headline PR and The Senior Executives of Take That Ltd. the book could not have been produced.

Finally, I dedicate the book to my parents, of whom I am a genetic derivative and who by example taught me to gear always on the upside.

Thankyou.
Stefan Bernstein, 2001

About the Author

The author is a registered representative of the Stock Exchange and a founder member of the Institute of Financial Planning. In addition, he is a qualified tax consultant with practices in London and Wiltshire. He advises corporations and individuals on their financial planning strategies.

Preface

A 'derivative' is simply a financial instrument derived from an underlying asset or stock.

This book explains in layman's terms, and with worked examples, each of the major derivatives and how they function.

Not only will the complete beginner gain an understanding of the various markets and opportunities that exist for trading, but more sophisticated investors should learn enough to consider derivatives for their own account.

Even if you choose not to venture into the derivatives market on your own, you will at least be able to judge if investments being made on your behalf are in safe hands. *Indeed, anyone with a pension, a mortgage or even a bank account cannot afford to turn a blind eye to derivatives.*

You will find a great many worked examples of traded options, futures, swaps, caps, collars and currency instruments. Each is presented clearly and avoids the unnecessary complexity, which market sentiment or other intangible factors might bring to the equation - though these factors are nonetheless debated separately for the sake of completeness so as not to obscure the main issues at stake.

Once the basics of each financial instrument have been covered, derivative concepts are expanded into specific case studies. These show how private traders and professionals alike could use combinations of individual instruments to achieve a particular effect.

Painting the full picture in a such a manner makes it easier to understand what each party's motives and obligations are, the risk/reward ratio involved in each transaction, and how simple models are constructed to track the progress of an investment.

Throughout the book you'll see just how easily very large amounts of money can be made in the various derivative markets. So, to balance the picture, there is a chapter devoted to the effects of getting derivatives trading wrong, based on certain high profile events over the last few years.

Obviously an '*Understand in a Day*' book can only give you an overview of the subject, and you should seek more in-depth advice before trading derivatives yourself.

$$\frac{\partial^2 C}{\partial \Sigma . \partial \sigma}$$

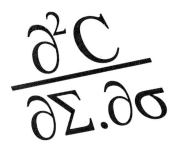

Introduction

A derivative is nothing more than
a financial instrument derived from
an underlying asset or stock,
often referred to as "the underlying".

Instead of trading in a stock itself, such as Microsoft or British Telecom shares, you simply trade in the appropriate derivative instruments. In other words, rather than buying Microsoft shares for $100 each or British Telecom shares for £8, you take out options (for perhaps $5 a share or 20p per share) to buy them at a later date. If the underlying share price increases during that period, then your $5 or 20p would be well spent and you will make more profit than if you'd bought the original shares. Therefore, derivative trading allows you to trade on a much-reduced level, and participate in gains on a much-increased level.

There are two sets of people who require derivatives, and these are the "hedgers" and the "traders". Each party has different motives, and each has developed the market in different directions.

A hedger is somebody with a "position" which he or she would like to cover. For example, an individual might have a large financial loan and would not like to be exposed to rising interest rates. He would therefore buy a "cap" (explained later). He is trading in the derivative, not the actual stock - if he were to trade in the stock, he would have bought an equivalent deposit, so that if rates rose, he would benefit from rising rates on that deposit to compensate for rising loan costs.

In this example, he cannot, of course, simply go out and buy a deposit otherwise he would be using the money that he had borrowed in the first place! So he has, instead, chosen a financial instrument derived from the deposit or loan to provide cover for the original position.

A trader has different motives. In the first place, he may have no actual position requiring a hedge, but would simply gamble on financial instruments like shares, currencies and interest rates to exploit the opportunities that occasionally arise.

'Arbitrage' is a trading technique designed to exploit pricing anomalies within markets or between different markets. It is possible that the same stock will be priced differently in two markets, at the same time, thus allowing a small profit on the differential between these two prices.

Different prices can arise for several reasons. For example, imagine somebody has an order to buy 1,000 shares. The market would easily fulfill it. But an order for several million shares would drive up the price. Accordingly, by fulfilling the small order in the knowledge of the large order, a significant profit can be made. Similarly, supply and demand can affect a stock price and the derivative price. In one market fixed rate dollar deposits might be sought after, and not so sought after in another. By taking a global view, the difference in prices may be arbitraged.

Clearly, hedgers have a real problem to solve and are therefore forced into the market. Traders, on the other hand, are merely in it out of choice, and they are looking for profit. However, they contribute to the market because they provide real liquidity. If traders didn't exist, hedgers would need to seek out counter-parties with opposite positions and carry out matched bargains. This would be rare and difficult, and there would be credit risks involved by using third parties directly, rather than a proper exchange.

But Why Bother?

It is the "gearing effect" that is so attractive to derivative traders. This effect can magnify differences, making the tiniest differential significant, and magnifying profits and losses enormously.

Imagine you have a bicycle and the pedal cog has 32 teeth. If the cog on the back wheel has 32 teeth as well, for each turn of the pedals there will be one full turn of the back wheel. If you now change the gear on the back wheel to a 16-tooth cog, then for every turn of the pedals there will be two turns in the back wheel,

One turn of the pedal = one turn of the wheel

One turn of the pedal = two turns of the wheel

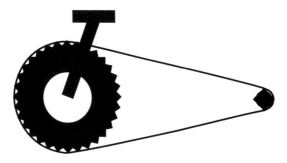

One turn of the pedal = eight turns of the wheel

and the bike should go twice as fast. If you change to a very small cog with only four teeth, then you should go eight times as fast as in the first example.

Leaving aside the engineering and physical problems of riding such a bike, the principle is clear - that the same amount of movement on the pedal cog can have a greater or lesser effect as a result of gearing.

Taking a financial example, imagine you put £1 as a bet on a horse at 50-1, details aside, you would expect to win £50. As the odds

---

shorten to, say, 10-1, then people who place their bets later would get a diminished return. You have both laid the same stake money, but your gearing effect is better.

Most people have experience of gearing without perhaps knowing it when they have bought their family home. Imagine one homeowner has a $10,000 deposit and a $90,000 loan on his home. His brother has a $90,000 deposit and a $10,000 loan. If each house rises in value to $200,000, then the first brother has made $100,000 on a $10,000 investment! His brother has made only $100,000 on a $90,000 investment. One has made 1,000%, whilst the other has made only 111%. This comes about as a result of the gearing involved in structuring the purchase of a house with a high loan-to-value ratio.

And that is the point - thousands of percentage points of profit can be made in the derivatives market.

From that point of view, it is a highly sophisticated and regulated casino, where the players battle one another without there necessarily being a "house" or "banker" to stack the odds. But the reality is this - anything that can rise by many thousand percent, can fall by a similar amount. This is what makes derivative trading so exciting and dangerous - it is a massive boom or bust opportunity and those who win, win heavily, whilst those who lose can be wiped out.

How It All Happens

Most exchanges have, or are in the process of, transferring all their derivatives trades to a computer based system. Those who were first to go 'electronic' have benefited from the move. For example, Eurex Deutschland in Frankfurt was able to steal virtually all the futures trading in bunds (German Government bonds) from under the noses of LIFFE (The London International Financial Futures and Options Exchange).

There are many arguments for and against screen trading compared to open outcry (person-to-person floor trading). Most are irrelevant to the average investor and affect only those closely linked to an exchange. But the most important is the affect on volatility.

Screen trading allows deals to be matched very quickly and extremely efficiently. Everyone can see what's going on at any one time. As a trader, you don't have to over-hear a deal between two other traders in the same pit to know what prices they've agreed. You can see it on screen, and mark your own prices accordingly. This means that the prices will stay within a tighter range since less 'mistakes' will be made, thus decreasing volatility. This, in turn, affects the pricing of options and other futures instruments.

It will take time before all exchanges around the world are fully converted to screen-based trading systems for all commodities, both financial and physical. Until that time, you should be aware of a few of the basics of pit trading.

The Trading Pit

This is the very hub of the old trading process. The examples in the next few sections were taken from the Chicago Mercantile Exchange (CME), although there is much in common between all the different exchanges.

There is basically one trading 'pit' or area for each commodity traded. When you see traders' frantic behaviour on news programmes in these pits, all they are doing is carrying out a process of constant bidding and offering of prices in the market.

Whilst the whole thing might look like a free for all, it is in fact very orderly with an agreed hand-signal language used in addition to shouting. Palms can be turned one way or the other to indicate an offer to buy or sell, fingers can be curled or straightened to indicate calls and puts, and the number of fingers used indicate the prices. Hands held near the face or head generally indicate volume.

Uniforms

One of the most distinctive features of the trading pit are the different colours of jacket which the traders and other individuals wear. This is a simple and quick way of identifying who is who.

Members or brokers generally wear **red** jackets and these are the individuals who execute trades.

Gold jackets are worn by runners, who get orders to the right broker in the pit as quickly as they can.

Pale green jackets are worn by "out-trade clerks" and they sort out any difficulties that may have arisen in previous trading, and which may not be resolved.

Orange jackets are worn by CME members whose main area of trade is emerging market futures.

Light blue jackets are worn by market reporters, who observe the pit and are employed by the CME. It is their job to note the prices at which trades are being executed, and then make sure the information is entered into the CME's own electronic pricing system. Of course, this information may then be relayed throughout the world.

All **other colours** and combinations of colours are used by individual firms or companies who trade on the floor - rather like the colours used by jockeys to indicate their stable.

Many people say that the "open outcry" markets will soon be a thing of the past. Computers are everywhere, in every walk of life and derivatives trading is no different. In many ways, this is the clash of tradition with modernity. The more traditional markets are used to open outcry trading and some individuals have spent a lifetime in the market. They know one another, and the market has a very personal dynamic. However, more modern markets, for example those opening up in Eastern Europe, necessarily start from the point of view of using the latest technology. Morcover, one can trade remotely via the Internet and other telecommunication systems, without the need to ever visit a trading floor.

On of the most exciting predictions for some is that if everything is to be done by screen, then it does not matter where the deal is "executed". The whole process could be a virtual deal taking place in cyberspace. As long as currencies are standardised, or at least rates of exchange agreed, then the whole thing can happen from your living room to someone else's kitchen table without the need for physical intervention at all.

Of course, this leads to enormous risks. In the traditional market, the clearinghouses' effectively-pooled assets provide a means of offering financial stability to underlying transactions on the exchange. If the trading environment is completely electronic, then those firms might not exist. So there could be an adverse effect on liquidity. However, it is hard to see how traders will be allowed to function without some means of depositing margins.

Another considerable danger would be a lack of regulations. At present, markets are heavily regulated. For example, it was the USA Commodities Futures Trading Commission that took proceedings against Sumitomo. If an organisation is regulated then it can be fined or closed down by the regulators. However, if trading is unregulated then how will anybody enforce the law? Traders could build up enormous losses that they simply could not sustain, with no underlying margin or safety net for the defrauded or misled counter-party.

Finally, there is the romantic view that the sight of hundreds of individuals jostling for position shouting and using arcane hand signals whilst all dressed in brightly coloured jackets is almost a tourist attraction in itself. I can remember when the UK stock exchange floor closed and an exciting and vibrant environment where individuals still wore bowler hats and top hats, disappeared overnight. The trading stands turned into coffeehouses and trading activity became nothing more than row on row of stripy shirted gentlemen staring at computer monitors. The derivatives market will go the same way - but that is progress.

Chapter One

Traded Options

Imagine there is a field next door to your home. A farmer owns it and if he were to sell it with planning permission for residential homes, it might be worth $1 million. However, the farmer wants money now and you want to guard against this development in the future (hedger) or to profit from the deal (trader).

You therefore buy an option from the farmer for $10,000. The terms of the option are that at any time in the next five years you may "exercise" your option, and therefore buy the field for a further $50,000 - the exercise or 'strike price'. If you do not exercise this option, then your basic stake money will be lost.

Imagine, then, that planning permission becomes very likely. You could then exercise your option (right to buy), thus buying the land for $50,000 and selling on immediately for the $1 million mentioned above. Your $10,000 has therefore developed into a 9,900% profit.

Now imagine that other homeowners and farmers were trading in land and the options "written" on land. You could have a recognised market enabling you to sell the option during the five year period irrespective of planning permission.

The option you bought was initially worth only $10,000 (being the price you paid for it) but over the period of five years it would fall in value as time elapsed because the opportunity for planning permission to be granted is becoming smaller. Alternatively, the option could become far more valuable if planning consent became more likely with changes in local policy. The "time value" and the "market factors" therefore, will affect the price at which you can trade the option.

The example above describes the theory behind a basic "call option" and the rest of this chapter considers these options and other straightforward instruments in greater depth. The examples are largely simplified and ignore dealing costs and market spreads. If you would like more detailed information, please see *Investing in Traded Options*, a hardback book by Robert Linggard and also published by TTL.

Call Options

These are basically the right to buy an asset at a specified price in the future. You would want to buy such an option if you thought that the price of the asset was going to rise.

For example, imagine it is June and that British Telecom Shares are £6. You suspect that the price might rise to £8 over the next six months but do not have the money to buy the shares at present. You might then buy a "British Telecom £6 December Call". Imagine that this costs you 20 pence. If the shares rise above £6.20 you are "in the money" i.e. in a position where you could exercise the option, buy the shares at £6 and sell them at £6.20 thus "closing out" your position at no loss.

If the shares rise to £7 you can now exercise your option at £6, buying the shares and immediately selling them for £1 profit. You would then make 80 pence on your 20 pence stake, a gain of 400%.

It is important to notice that even though the shares rose by only £1, or 16.6%, you made 400%.

Of course, if the shares did not rise by at least 20 pence your option would expire as worthless in December and you would have lost all your stake money.

As time goes by, therefore, the value of an option would decline (there being less time or 'chance' of the underlying price rising), all other things being equal, as in the graph below:-

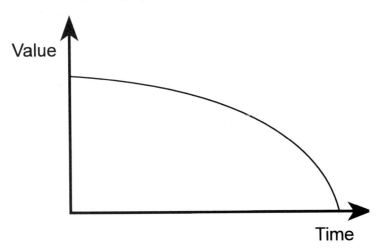

Of course, there could be other factors that affect the value of the option. Imagine for example that during the six month period there was a crash in Telecom shares or the market in general, followed by a major recovery. Then the value graph might look like the one below:-

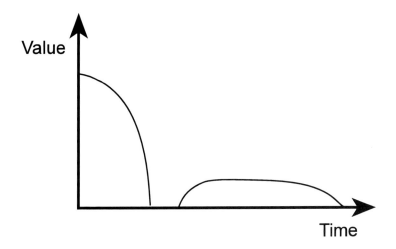

You do not need to stay with an option simply because you have bought it. Many people trade options quite actively and will sometimes buy and sell the same classes of option many times on the same day depending on minute underlying market movements which are always magnified by the "gearing" effect of options.

Put Options

This is the right to sell an asset at a specific price at a pre-determined time in the future or at any time leading up to that date. Imagine therefore, that you are a holder of Telecom shares and you think they are fully valued at £6. You would buy an option that allowed you to sell them at £6 at any time in the next six months. If of course, the crash happens and the price falls then your option will be in the money. You would then be able to exercise your option and require the other party to buy your shares at £6. If you wanted to, you could use the proceeds to buy back the shares at the reduced price.

Once again, the same factors apply in terms of distorting the value of the option over time and due to market movements. Of course, should the shares rise then you would never exercise the option because you would not wish to sell, and once again all your stake money would be lost.

Writing Options

So far the examples of both Put and Call Options have concerned the purchase and sale of options. In these cases all that you can lose is the money you have spent on the options - your stake money or "option premium". There is a good chance that you might make a gain, but your biggest potential loss is the amount you have spent.

An alternative to this is to actually "write" the options. This means you act as the 'other party' in the above transactions and it carries a great deal more risk.

For example, imagine you write a Call Option allowing someone the right to buy British Telecom at £6 at any time in the next six months. The option premium you receive is 40 pence a share. If the shares rise to £10 then you would undoubtedly be "exercised" and would have to go into the market to buy the shares at £10 and sell them at £6. You would have lost £4 per share, or TEN TIMES your original premium!

All you need to do is magnify this across a 'wonder' stock, such as the 10p share that suddenly rises to over a £5, and the percentage losses can be dramatic. The graph below shows how the option price might rise in line with a rising stock price:-

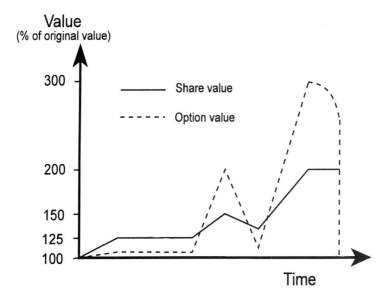

If you were writing a Put Option you would, in the worst scenario, be giving the other party the right to dump stock on you at a price much higher than the current market price. You would have to find the money to buy that stock which you would then probably have to re-sell immediately and take the loss.

The risk in this sense is quantifiable because the stock cannot go below "0 pence". So in the Telecom example, you cannot lose more than fifteen times your original notional profit. Whereas on the up side the losses are effectively unlimited.

Option Jargon

At The Money
This is a phrase used to describe an Option whose exercise price is equal to the current market price.

Out of The Money
This is a phrase used to describe an Option when the exercise price is less favourable to the Option holder than the current market price. The Option holder would not therefore exercise the Option which has no real value.

In The Money
This describes an Option when the exercise price is more favourable to the Option holder than the current market value. An Option such as this has real value and is likely to be excercised.

Premium
It is normally necessary to pay the Option premium in full when the Option is purchased. Some markets do not require a full settlement however, until the Option is exercised or reaches its expiry date. Before that date the buyer need only pay a fraction of the premium which is known as a "margin". As the Option moves out of the money, further margin must be paid, known as "variation margin". This is a very useful benefit for Option purchasers, who do not therefore need to pay a full price of Options if they are trading actively.

Margin
There is an initial margin and a variation margin. The variation margin is explained above and changes in value as each day goes by.

The Risk Factor

This is an expression of a movement in the price of an Option as a result of the movement in the price of the underlying stock, or instrument to which it refers.

Over-the-Counter Options

Not all Options are Traded Options, run through a recognised exchange, as the example of the farmer's field shows. There may be matched deals or bespoke contracts created for a particular purpose. In this case, the purchaser of the Option is taking something of a credit risk and there is also danger in terms of liquidity. For example, if markets develop and go against the Option holder, it is not as easy to close out the Option as it would be in the liquid Traded Options Market. Moreover, there is unlikely to be a contract available to purchase against an open position if the original contract was highly personalised (nobody wants the field).

American Options

An option that may be exercised at any time up to and including the expiry date. These options allow the holder to take a notional profit (or loss) at any stage.

European Option

An option that may only be exercised on the expiry date. The holder is, therefore, unable to benefit from any favourable price movements of the underlying during the option's lifetime.

Break Forwards

These are a relatively recent creation which allow the purchaser more flexibility. The basic principle is that a contract is made but it can be broken on terms agreed with the Option writer if the circumstances are appropriate. An Option purchaser might choose a fixed rate for the future, but see that the current spot rate or another forward rate is more favourable. He would then unwind the contract and re-think his position or simply repurchase on different terms. This can be very useful for those people who trade across borders. For example, imagine a German company is receiving sterling for a contract six months in the future. In order to guard against the weakening of sterling they buy an F.X. Option contract. However, during the term of the contract, sterling becomes stronger and stronger. They would "break forward" on the contract and simply take the profit brought about by sterling having strengthened.

Participating Forwards

These contracts allow the buyer to participate in the upside of the contract. It would suit those people who think that they might have a potential upside in their currency exposure but whose prudence leads them to buy protection against any down side.

As a consequence of having taken an effectively double position, the buyer of the Option would not participate in the full upside of the deal.

Imagine, in the break forward example above, that the company had agreed a floor in case sterling weakened considerably, but in the belief that sterling might rise agreed a participation level of say 70% of that rise. They would then be covered against the adverse consequences of sterling's fall, and at the same time be allowed to participate in sterling's rise, although to a limited extent.

Pricing Options

Even in the world of derivatives the mathematics used to price options is complex. The laws of supply and demand, and the background effects of exchange rates and interest rates are only part of the story. The main reason is that, unlike normal equities, options involve a certain degree of prediction of future events. So, on top of supply and demand, options need to take into account:

- What the option is for,
- How the strike price relates to the underlying,
- The time to expiry,
- Interest rates, and most importantly
- Volatility.

The combination of all these factors requires the use of a complex set of equations to form a model. These models are then used to set the price of options. Of course, they have been developed over long periods and adjustments have been made to the models whenever errors have been spotted. By now the pricing of options is a fairly mature science and options are priced correctly the majority of the time.

Option Details

It may sound obvious but the first factor to consider in the pricing of an option is what the option is for. Is it an option to buy or to sell? Is it an option on a call or a put? Is it a European or American?

For example, an American style option, which can be exercised at any time up to the expiry date, will be more expensive than a European style option on the same underlying with the same strike price and expiry date. This is because there is more uncertainty on behalf of the seller as to whether the option will be exercised or not, and so the seller will need to be compensated for this increased risk.

Strike Price and Underlying Price

The price of the option is closely connected to the relationship between the strike price and the price of the underlying financial instrument. Obviously an option to buy a commodity at the price of 100, when the underlying price is 90, is more valuable than an option to buy at a strike price of 200.

Essentially the relationship between the strike price and the value of the underlying reflects itself in the price of an option in two ways; the "inherent" or "intrinsic" value, and the "time" or "extrinsic" value.

The right to buy at a price of 100, when the underlying price is 120, is obviously worth at least 20. This is because the option, if exercised, would already be profitable by that amount. This is the **intrinsic value** of the option.

The same option may still have a period to run before the expiry date. During this time the underlying may rise even further and increase the profit on the option. The chance that this underlying price will increase further has to be worth a certain amount and could be, say, another 20 on the price. This element of the option's price is known as the **time value**.

If the price of the underlying, in the above example, had only been 90, then the option to buy at a hundred would have no intrinsic value. If it were not for the time value then this option would be worthless. However there will be a chance that the price will rise above the strike price before the expiry date and this will give it a value to the market.

In summary:

In-the-money options have intrinsic value and time value. The price of an in-the-money option will usually reflect somewhere between half and the full amount of changes in the underlying price.

At-the-money options only have time value. The price of at-the-money options will generally show a change of around 50% of the change in the underlying.

Out-of-the-money options have time values which are decreased in proportion to the amount by which they are out-of-the-money. The price of out-of-the-money options can reflect from 0% to half of the change in the underlying.

Generally speaking the longer the time to expiry for the option the higher the premium that will be placed on it by the seller. This is to compensate them for the higher risk that it could prove profitable to the buyer. The rate of decrease of the time value, known as "time decay", is not linear and it accelerates quite rapidly as the option nears expiry. This behaviour, shown on page 19 works against the interests of buyers and in favour of sellers.

Interest Rates

Interest rates have a relatively small impact on the pricing of options compared to forwards and futures. The only reason it appears in options pricing models is because the seller is able to place the premium in a risk free investment and therefore receive a coupon.

Volatility

Volatility is the most single important factor when it comes to pricing options correctly. Indeed, many currency options have their prices quoted in terms of volatility.

The volatility of the underlying price is calculated using various statistical techniques on historical data. Although this is not ideal, because it is "historic", it is the only alternative to second-guessing the fundamentals.

For underlying instruments with high volatility it will prove more costly for sellers to hedge themselves against the risks incurred from writing the relevant options. Therefore they will require a greater premium for this increased risk which will reflect itself in a higher cost for the option. If the market believes that a market maker has set their option prices too low they will find that they will end up selling options to meet the high demand until they increase their prices to a level where the market thinks is fair. Similarly if the price is set too high they will be sold options until they reduce their prices into line with expectations of the market. So it could be said that the supply and demand of the markets will always reflect a market "consensus" of the predicted volatility. Nevertheless, the market will never be entirely correct (or very rarely) and this is where significant profits can be made.

Changes in the volatility of an underlying will have a different impact on the price of an option depending on whether it is in-the-money, at-the-money or out-of-the-money. In-the-money options will only show a relatively small change in price corresponding to a change in the volatility of the underlying. Whereas at-the-money options will show a directly proportionate change in their value. Out-of-the-money options, on the other hand, can show wild fluctuations depending on how far they are out-of-the-money. If an option is only just out-of-the-money and the volatility increases by just a small amount this can have a huge affect on the price of the option. A change of just 5-10% in the volatility could mean that the option price moving by up to 50% or more.

As you can see the pricing of options is an extremely complex matter. It is impossible to look at an underlying instrument and then work out the price of relevant options in your head. You can see from the above factors that it is very possible that you may buy a call in a commodity when you think that its price is going to increase. Yet you could end up showing a loss despite the value of the commodity rising. This could be because the rise would be too small over the time that it took to increase, or that there had been a significant decrease in the volatility.

Summary

Traded options offer a very useful way of :-

1.   Hedging current portfolios against market movements.

2.   Making extra income from existing portfolios.

3.   Participating in the Stock Market at a reduced stake but with greatly increased risk.

Most U.K. & U.S. Stockbrokers are happy to run traded option accounts for experienced investors who are willing to understand the risks, sign the necessary disclaimers, and put up the relevant margins (see later).

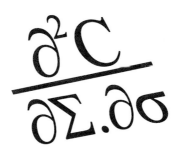

$$\frac{\partial^2 C}{\partial \Sigma . \partial \sigma}$$

Chapter Two

Futures

A Futures contract is basically an agreement to deliver a set quantity of a particular commodity at a pre-agreed price on a date in the future. These dates are usually the quarter dates of March, June, September and December.

There are several exchanges in New York, Tokyo, London, and of course, Chicago. In the UK, LIFFE (the London International Financial Futures and Options Exchange), acts as a clearing house and trading medium.

But why would anyone want to trade in a Futures contract in the first place? Well, imagine you are a farmer and that you can produce 10,000 tons of grain. Your production costs are $10 per ton, and the current price is $12 per ton. You know, therefore, that at the end of the harvest, barring accidents, you will be in profit to the tune of $2 a ton.

However, imagine there is a sudden glut of grain, and the price drops to $7 per ton. Now, you will not only fail to make a profit, but you will have to sell your grain at a considerable loss. It would have been better not to harvest it at all because then you wouldn't have lost the $3 a ton in this example.

The answer lies in your selling the grain forward with a Futures contract. You would lock in to the $12 a ton rate quoted today for your future delivery date. Buying the contract would eat into your $2 profit, but at least some profit is better than none, or a massive loss.

Commodities

By the mid nineteenth century, Chicago was already a major trading centre in America. This was largely due to the infrastructure of railways and telegraph connections. When the McCormick Reaper was invented the harvesting of wheat became much easier and led to an enormous increase in the amount of wheat produced. So mid-west farmers travelled to Chicago in order to sell their excess wheat and the dealers to whom they sold it then shipped it all over the country.

All this necessitated the creation of a centralised organisation where people could meet in order to deal in grain. It didn't take long before the (perhaps hard-up, perhaps greedy) farmers would commit themselves to deliver grain at sometime in the future. Of course, this is the start of commodities trading. (Some will argue that in Greek times the same process took place with rice and other crops, but this was much more an over-the-counter market with counterparties difficult to find. The Chicago exchange was probably the first real exchange that had all the necessary features, namely a liquid market, traders on both sides, hedgers, and arbitrageurs.)

The Advantages

The advantage to the farmers of this way of trading was enormous. They knew the price at which they had to sell their wheat in order to make a profit and being able to lock into that price in advance was sometimes the only thing that kept them afloat. Of course, if the price were to rise they would lose the extra profit, but at least they would be certain that they could definitely sell the wheat they had harvested.

As the market became more sophisticated, formal contracts were written and banks would lend on those contracts. Moreover, traders were able to sell contracts on to other traders who had different positions.

On the other side of the fence, the farmers also began to buy and sell contracts based on their obligations to deliver. For example, one farmer may have had a poor crop and found himself short of wheat, whilst another may have produced more than he actually had contracts for. It would be simple to put a deal together to satisfy both parties before they went to the market.

Before long, contracts were being sold to counterparties who had no intention of ever taking delivery of the wheat.

These days the markets are now extremely sophisticated with a variety of different instruments and contracts available, denominated in several major currencies and with a wide variety of underlying commodities.

The Participants

Once again there are hedgers, traders and arbitrageurs.

The hedger is someone with a particular position in a physical commodity who is trying to safeguard that position. Take beef for example. The breeding cycle of cows is no short-term matter. Accordingly, investment has to be made based on future assumptions. To be able to lock into those assumptions gives the farmer a degree of certainty.

Another hedger would be somebody who actually must own a particular commodity in order to continue to trade. Sumitomo (see 'When it all goes wrong') is a good example, because they physically manufacture batteries and therefore require the actual copper in question.

The traders have no physical position in any commodities and just simply want to exploit the differences in supply and demand, currency differences or differences between different markets in different geographical locations.

Arbitrageurs are trading simply to exploit these differences. For example, with the advent of global and instantaneous trading, it might be possible to spot a difference between the price of a particular futures contract in different markets. By shorting one and going long on another, the overall effect might be that contracts cancel out and still have a profitable margin.

Many people see hedgers as the more legitimate party. The truth is however, that without the traders, hedgers would be unable to hedge. Traders provide the liquidity in the market because they will trade in almost any commodity and in any contract format. Many professionals are wary of hedgers, because they have a genuine need to trade. So they will often hold a position with more tenacity than a trader because they are perhaps more deeply or personally affected by the result. This is an interesting and vital dynamic within the market.

So Where Is The Danger?

Of course the explanation above simply describes a liquid market in which all participants seem to be getting what they want. Real life is not so simple. If there is any sort of catastrophe, for example a war in the OPEC region, or bad weather in grain producing countries, then price moves can be dramatic. As intimated in chapter one, whilst the underlying price move might be 10% or 20%, the price move on a derivative contract could be denominated in thousands of percent. This is why traders get involved; derivatives dealing can give quite fantastic results. It can also result in catastrophic losses.

How a Commodities Trade Works

The format of an exchange-based trade is essentially a constant, whether an individual is trading for hedging reasons, speculating or arbitraging. Like any derivative market, there must be a clear agreement on what a particular contract will include.

You might decide to trade in grain. However, you will have to define the quantity of the grain, the delivery date, its price and its purity. All these features are standardised as far as possible so that everyone can move quickly without ever having to read the small print or send contracts off to lawyers. Such a delay would effectively kill the market. One party is trying to introduce a degree of certainty to the activities, whilst the other party might be looking to exploit uncertainty.

Imagine you are a speculator and you think that the price of gold is about to rocket because of difficulties in the gold producing regions. You would probably buy a futures contract and would therefore be taking a "long position".

Imagine for example, the current futures price for gold is £100 per contract. If, during the life of the contract, the price of the contract itself should rise to say, £150 due to the perceived shortages actually becoming real, then the contract holder would simply sell his contract at £150 having made a handsome 50% profit. This sort of profit could be made on an almost fractional increase in the price of gold, depending on the term of the contract and the amount of "underlying" to which it refers.

Of course, if the price goes the other way, because of increased production the speculator might find he can now sell his contract for only £50 and would therefore lose £50. Once again a fractional fall in price could bring this about.

Most of the successful traders recognise when events are going against them and learn to close out positions that are going wrong. When it comes to creating your own trading strategy, you need to learn this fundamental rule.

What makes commodities trading exchanges so flexible is that speculators do not need to take delivery of the hard commodity itself. Imagine how difficult it is to physically store grain, or the insurance requirements for storing precious metals. It is much simpler to be the holder of an abstract paper or electronic contract. Derivative contracts allow trading to be much simpler and immediate.

In the example above the most that could be lost was £100. This is hardly a serious issue for most investors. However, that was simply because the trader had bought a contract; with bought contracts, the most you can lose is your stake money. But, if you sell a contract in commodities, then the risk could be almost unlimited.

For example, imagine our speculator thought huge amounts of gold would be discovered and that this would halve the price. In this case he could go out and sell the contract he bought in the previous example for the same amount. Let's say he received £100 but now he is obliged to deliver the gold on a specified date. Because gold is going to collapse in price he knows he will be able to buy a contract to close out his position for £25. He will therefore make a very handsome profit.

Of course the danger is, that prices will move the other way. For example, if all the gold mines in the world suddenly discover that the gold they are mining today is the last they will ever find, the price would rocket. Before the trader could act, the price of the contract to close out his position might cost him £1,000 or even £10,000. If he buys a contract at £10,000 he has closed out his position completely but he has lost a hundred times his stake money! Such wild price fluctuations are not uncommon. Just look at the political instability in the Middle East that affects oil or the periodic stock market crashes all round the world.

So selling short is the most dangerous approach. This applies to all derivatives and even sometimes to the underlying commodity itself, or to shares or other physical assets. When you buy long, you know the price of the asset you have bought cannot fall below zero and so your total loss, if you are unable to trade and miss the price collapse, will be the money you staked (This could be geared in relation to your margin.)

By going short, however, you are obliged to deliver something you do not own and that you will therefore be obliged to buy whatever the price is. Prices could rise dramatically and so the risk of being wiped out by fluctuations is immense when selling short.

How a Trade is Executed

When there is so much at stake in terms of vast gains and potentially enormous losses, many people are surprised to discover how very simple it is to place an order once you are established with your trading account. There are many decisions like buying your home or a new car, where you are faced with masses of time-consuming paperwork and inherent delays in the process. In comparison with this, the placing of a commodities order could hardly be simpler.

Let's imagine for example, that your research tells you the price of oil will go down shortly. All you need do is call your broker's trading desk, identify yourself with your account number and ask to "sell one June oil contract at the market". Your broker will probably stay on the telephone for a few seconds before he confirms that the deal has now been done. The deal will be executed directly to the relevant trading floor within the relevant commodities exchange, either electronically or by the old-fashioned telephone method.

Your brokers response should then be that you have sold one June oil contract at $X per barrel. Even though you may have spent no more than a couple of minutes on the telephone, you are now on the hook for any potential rise in the price of oil. Imagine therefore that there is a shortage of oil (instead of the glut that you expected). The oil price may begin to rise beyond the price that you have paid. If you consider this to be a long-term trend (i.e. you have changed your mind), you will want to get out as quickly as possible. You will immediately telephone your broker and confirm that you would now like to buy one June oil contract at the market price. Once again, the deal can be done in a minute or so and you have now successfully closed your position, even though you may have lost a considerable amount of money.

In fact, as the day goes on, you may decide that the price of oil will continue to rise so you call your broker again, wanting to go along by purchasing another June contract.

Unfortunately, as the week wears on, you realise you were right in the first place and the price begins to slip! Now you have to call your broker again and sell short in order to close out the second position you created.

In total, you may have spent only ten minutes on the phone in the entire process, but you may have lost or made thousands of dollars.

Taking Delivery

Imagine you take out a long position in some commodity and choose not to close it, or you forget to do so. What happens then? If you've purchased 10 tons of coffee, could you expect some lorries to appear in the road, and promptly tip a mountain of caffeine on your drive the day after the contract expires? Well, before you go out and arrange your coffee mornings for the next 30 years, this won't happen.

This is where a good broker comes in useful. As your contract nears maturity, be it long or short, your broker's firm should be keeping a wary eye on it. Sometime before "delivery", the firm should telephone all open long position holders and tell them to either close their position or prepare to take full delivery. They will also have to pay the value of the underlying contract. Similarly, holders of open short contracts will be asked to close out their trades or make ready to deliver the underlying commodity (and actually demonstrate they have the required quantity and quality available for delivery).

Even if you were to leave your position open in order to take delivery, you would still not wake up with the aroma of freshly tipped coffee in your garden. Instead, what you would probably receive is a receipt entitling you to take your commodity from a warehouse or other distribution point. Financial commodities are an exception to this rule, because they don't actually exist.

Even manufacturers and processing companies who trade with commodities rarely take delivery of the underlying goods. This is because the commodity contracts may not necessarily be denominated in precisely the quantity or grade they need. In any event, the contracts are probably an abstract guarantee of some sort against the physical commodities they are holding, buying or selling. Instead, they will close their position, having successfully hedged against price movements so they can then go and carry out their transactions. Only those companies who trade in a commodity for which they can find buyers at many different grades tend to take physical delivery.

The Commodity Exchanges

All commodities exchanges work in a similar manner. The people trading must be members of the exchange itself. These members then support the exchange by paying dues and assessments. Ordinary individuals wishing to trade must do so through a broker who will employ officers who hold memberships.

The exchange doesn't just provide the physical location where trades can take place, but also related services. These can include communication systems, price reporting and information circulation systems. Employees of the exchange also keep an eye on the day-to-day operations to make sure the rules are adhered to. The exchange doesn't set the prices, nor does it buy or sell in its own right.

Each commodities exchange also has a clearing association that works in a similar manner to how a clearinghouse works with banks. Highly capitalised members of the exchange and various other corporations or partnerships (one of whose officials must be a member of the exchange, just like the UK stock exchange) make up the membership of the clearing association. Any members of the exchange who are not members of the clearing association can only clear their trades through those who are. The association's members have to put up a fixed original margin with a clearinghouse. They have to maintain this margin when price fluctuations go against them. The clearinghouse can call for further margin through the day instead of waiting for normal settlement at the end of the day, if it thinks that course of action is appropriate.

Financial Futures

There are three main types of Financial Futures contract:

1. Stock Index Futures
2. Interest Rate Futures
3. Currency Futures

A **Stock Index Future** is effectively a bet on an upward or downward movement in a particular Stock Market index, such as the FTSE Index in London or the Dow Jones in New York. A trader might decide that the index could fall dramatically if, for example, the latest Middle East peace process fails. He or she would therefore buy a contract allowing him to sell the index at the current value at a time in the future after the expected failure of the negotiations.

Perhaps, during the process, the situation might begin to look bleaker and bleaker, and so the contract could be sold out at a large short-term profit. Alternatively, the signs for peace might start to look increasingly positive, and the Futures contract might become worthless. To protect himself, a trader could have also purchased a Put Option, or indeed written both Put and Call Options to create a straddle.

Stock Index Futures allow the trader or the hedger to participate in the upward movement of stock markets at reduced cost. They also allow the hedger or trader to protect themselves, or even benefit from downward movements in the market.

Interest Rate Futures work in a similar fashion where the hedger would need to protect himself against major rises or falls in interest rates that could affect his business activities. Once again, the trader would simply be looking to profit opportunities created by temporary movements in the market. For example, if everyone is expecting interest rates to go from 8% to 9% to 10% over a six-month period, and there is an ERM style fiasco that drives interest rates to 15% temporarily, then the opportunities for trading profits will be immense, and the losses for those people with open positions would be similarly large.

Currency Futures protect a hedger against alterations in exchange rates that could affect the profitability of a particular project. For example, a business that is building a dam in Japan may be sourcing all its labour and materials in yen, but have its capital base and many of its borrowings in sterling. A problem it might face could be that of a strengthening yen to the extent that the capital available in sterling would be insufficient, to complete the job. Accordingly, a Futures contract might be helpful, to fix a known rate of exchange between sterling and the yen.

Futures can therefore be an important hedging mechanism for anyone trading in Global Markets, or anyone for whom currency movements, interest rate movements or stock market movements could mean a significant alteration to their profitability.

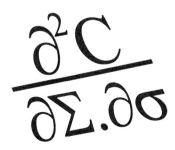

$$\frac{\partial^2 C}{\partial \Sigma . \partial \sigma}$$

Chapter Three

Swaps

S waps were born in the 1980s and they are now regulated by the British Bankers Association and the International Swap Dealers Association. The market is thought to be worth some $1.5 billion and includes both hedgers and active traders. There are both interest rate and currency swaps arising as a result of local differences in interest rate and currency markets, and differing credit ratings between various institutions involved.

The point is that one borrower in one market may have an advantage over another borrower does not have in that particular market. However, the second borrower may enjoy an advantage in their own market that is denied to the first borrower.

Example

Imagine that Tom is a lawyer and his bank will therefore give him a floating rate of 7% to buy his house. But the fixed rate they offer him is 11%. Joan, however, is not in favour with her bank, and they have offered her a floating rate of 10%. However, having been a long term Building Society customer, she has been offered 9% on a fixed basis. Tom thinks rates will go up, but Joan believes they are about to drop.

In this example, each party would borrow £100,000 to purchase their home, Tom floating at 7%, and Joan fixed at 9%. They would then effect an interest rate swap so that Tom ends up with 9% fixed, and Joan with 7% floating. Each party now has the borrowing profile which they require, and each is better off as a result of having swapped. Of course, this would never happen with individuals, but large corporations and banks have to carry out these transactions to survive.

Interest Rate Swaps

These are a means of changing the interest rate basis of debt without changing the underlying principal obligation. You might swap from fixed to floating, or the other way, as in the example of Tom and Joan. Lenders might not know that the swap has taken place and would still look to the original borrower for payment. This then means that each party is at risk that the other party in the transaction fails to meet its obligation. This credit risk is often unacceptable and leads to the double swap.

The Double Swap

This arises if one or both parties are not keen on the risk involved with the counter-party. They would therefore go through a third party such as a bank. In this case, each individual party deals direct with the bank and may not be aware of the other party's identity.

The bank in the middle guarantees each party's performance and accordingly takes a fee. The fee comes off the arbitrage profit, but both parties should still be ahead.

In the example of Tom and Joan above, each might have gone through a bank that could have charged a half-percent facility fee to each. Even having paid that, both borrowers had a better rate than they would otherwise have been able to achieve, had it not been for the swap.

Capital Market Anomalies

Certain institutions, such as banks, can borrow at fixed rates, which is generally seen as a sign of quality. Industrial concerns mainly have to concentrate on floating rates. Moreover, an organisation that is well known in a particular market, for example, the largest company in a particular country's stock exchange, may have a poorer rating in a foreign country than it has at home.

In this case, the resident company might have access to its own currency on better rates than the foreign company. This would be another reason for effecting a swap. Each would borrow at preferential rates in its own country, and perhaps in its own currency, and then effect swaps.

Market Conditions

It could, of course, be that one type of lending is in short supply. Imagine, for example, if there is upward pressure on interest rates, fixed rates may be difficult to come by. In another market perhaps, there is downward pressure on interest rates so that fixed rates are plentiful. This would be another motive for effecting an interest rate swap.

Basis Rate Swaps

In the various international markets there are different methods of fixing interest rates and calculating "base". There is the US dollar prime rate, the US dollar Libor (London Inter-Bank Offered Rate), the US dollar commercial paper, the UK Sterling Libor rate, etc.

Not only is "base" calculated differently, but the payment of interest is calculated distinctly too. Finally, there are different methods of calculating the number of days in the year! Whilst there are 365 in the US, there are only 360 in Europe!

Clearly, with differences in the calculation of the "base", differing payment dates, and differing numbers of days in a year, there is a considerable opportunity for traders to arbitrage such situations and make money on the margins.

Summary

The Swaps market offers the following opportunities.

1. Traders can arbitrage between various market differentials.
2. Industrial corporations may have access to markets, which would otherwise be denied.
3. Industrial corporations could have access to terms, which would otherwise be unavailable.
4. Industrial corporations can convert debt from fixed to floating and vice-versa for reasons of treasury management.

If you are interested in learning more about Swaps and the Swaps markets, please see *Understand Swaps in a Day* by Terry Carroll, also published by TTL.

Chapter Four

More Derivatives

Currency Exchange Agreements

Currency Exchange agreements differ from Swaps because the principal (original loan) is exchanged, so this is basically a Foreign Exchange deal. The first of these were carried out by IBM and The World Bank in the 1980s, and the market has grown significantly since.

Imagine UK Cars Ltd is doing well in Germany. UK Computers Ltd, however, has a great profile in the United States. But, UK Cars Ltd wants dollars, and UK Computers Ltd needs Deutsch Marks. The answer to this problem is that UK Cars Ltd would borrow in Deutschmarks at a very competitive rate. UK Computers, however, would borrow in dollars at a very competitive rate. They would then swap both the principal and the interest, thus transferring the whole obligation over to the other party.

The effect is likely to be that they are both paying less and have achieved the borrowing, both as to principal and interest rate payments, that they require for the businesses to function successfully.

Once again, if each borrower is concerned with the other's covenant, then a third party may be interposed. At the end of the contract, the entire principal should be exchanged and each borrower pays off their obligation as appropriate.

Of course, examples can become much more complex where not just the currencies are involved, but different rates. For example, one corporation may need a fixed rate of 10% on dollars, whilst the other would like a floating Libor + 3 on sterling. The netting off of the different payments which must flow between the two corporations to meet their obligations can be complex, and this is where a third party clearinghouse activity would be welcome.

Currency Exchange agreements therefore offer the following:

1. The opportunity to obtain a loan in a currency that might not otherwise be available.

2. The opportunity to hedge foreign currency risk.

3. The opportunity to exploit favourable conditions in certain markets.

Deposit Swaps

This takes the idea of Swaps and currency exchange agreements further. Factors such as inflation, or supply and demand, can lead to distortions between interest rates on a particular currency in different countries or markets. One market might rate the dollar at 150 against sterling, whilst another rates it at 149.5. This offers an opportunity to make an arbitrage profit on the difference.

Imagine that the sterling deposit rate is 10%, and that the bank offering that rate can lend on at 12%. There is a clear 2% margin on the activity. However, perhaps the lending rate in Germany is 13% in Deutsch Marks. The bank might then convert its cash deposits to Deutsch Marks, and lend them in Germany. At the end of the term it would convert back the principal to the original currency and close out the whole deal. Whilst in this example a 1% interest rate improvement has been effected, this is 50% more profit than would otherwise have been made.

Naturally, there is a risk involved in this. Imagine that the Deutsch Mark weakens dramatically against the pound. If it began at three Deutsch Marks per pound and ends the term of the loan at four Deutsch Marks per pound then there will be a 33% shortfall in the repayment proceeds. Of course, any prudent bank would hedge the foreign exchange risk with an Option or a Futures contract.

Future Rate Agreements

Many institutions need to manage their interest rate exposure for a particular period, but wish to do so without a loan or deposit. For example, if you think that rates will rise, then you might make a deposit. If you think they will fall, then you might borrow money. However it is both expensive and requires a lot of capital, so Future Rate Agreements, (FRAs) are used to remove the effect of interest rate volatility.

An institution seeking to protect itself against interest rates rising would buy a FRA, whereas an institution wishing to protect itself against falling rates might sell one.

The market for the FRA is effectively through banks that sell them as over-the-counter instruments.

As with most derivative instruments, these can be used simply as a means of hedging a genuine commitment, or purely for trading purposes. FRAs are available in a variety of major currencies to satisfy the requirements of those institutions with an international perspective.

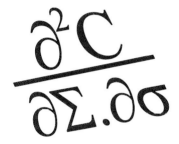

$$\frac{\partial^2 C}{\partial \Sigma . \partial \sigma}$$

Chapter Five

More Complex Derivative Models & Strategies

So far we've only covered the basics of derivatives, and some would say that is enough to actively trade in the market should you wish. However, the life of the professional derivative trader or hedger is much more complex. Whether this complexity is necessary, or whether it is merely a smoke screen created to deter the masses from their 'patch' is open for debate. Nevertheless, here are some of the more common models and strategies adopted in those circles...

Chartists

In all of the world's stock markets, there are bodies of people known as "chartists" or technical analysts. They follow market trends and seek to create a chart or a series of geometric patterns from price movements. They believe that by creating these charts they will be able to extend the lines of a particular geometric pattern and that this will help to indicate the direction in which the market is going.

The simplest example of this would be when chartists plot a stock market movement within a set of parallel lines as in the example below.

**Market
Value**

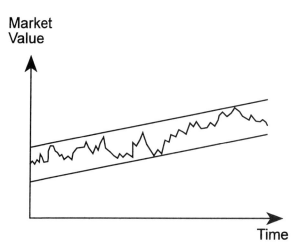

Time

The market has been working in a particular trading range and has not broken out. The inference therefore is that it should remain in that trading range and rise gradually. However, in the example below, the market has broken through the trading range, which is known as a "chart breakout". What this means is that there will now be a new trading range established after a few days.

**Market
Value**

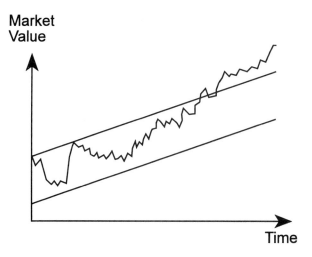

Time

There are those who believe in technical analysis implicitly, but there are a great many people who consider the whole idea to be nonsense. How can a trading medium as dynamic as the stock market have its upward and downward progress indicated by lines superimposed on a trading pattern? Surely economic events would move the markets, rather than the markets conform to patterns to which it cannot be linked in any way (other than through the imposition and creation of those patterns).

However, because of sentiment, the whole idea of technical analysis is self-fulfilling. For example, once the market breaks through the trading range as a chart breakout, all the chartists may consider this a buying signal. The rest of the traders may therefore have to buy, simply because of the weight of the money from technical analysts will move the market anyway.

In this way, a trading model can function at two levels. On the one hand it can be a mechanism that accurately predicts the market, and on the other level an instrument which, because it is thought able to predict the market, can somehow dictate its future movements.

Options traders are particularly fond of charting techniques. The purchase of the correct option at the right time can be used to protect a position should the trend be unexpectedly broken, and to magnify profits when the expected movements occur (most likely brought about by pre-programmed computer trades).

The Tarantula

The purpose of a tarantula is to produce an overall profit from a diverse book of derivative contracts.

To keep the example simple, imagine that there is an eight-legged spider where the tip of the leg to the spider's body represents the lapse of time. Additionally, each leg represents a different Futures or Options contract in eight major currencies, the U.S. Dollar, Sterling, the Deutsch Mark, Swiss Francs, the Yen, Hong Kong Dollars, French Francs, and the Peseta.

If contracts are affected on each of the "legs", then they will vary in value with currency fluctuations from the tip of the leg to the body of the spider. Each trader will write a line, either on a common spider as a syndicate, or on his own spider. He will write a line on each leg and, depending how he feels about a particular currency, this will be a white line or a black line. White lines are written on legs where the trader is Bullish about the currency, and black lines are when the trader is Bearish.

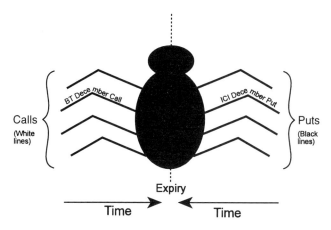

A tarantula then will be comprised of eight similar contracts all expiring on the same date and will have several white and several black legs, depending on the trader's views and on the current currency relationships.

Imagine, now, that the U.S Dollar on one spider's leg were a white line. Unfortunately, the Dollar collapses so that the leg becomes worthless. This is known as a "broken leg". If the collapse happens early on up the leg, with plenty of time left to expiry, then there is a prospect of "healing". But, if the leg is broken close to the body, this is far less likely. If a spider has less than three broken legs, it is known as a crippled spider because the likelihood for profit is now so greatly reduced. If a spider has four or more broken legs, then it is said to be "deaf".

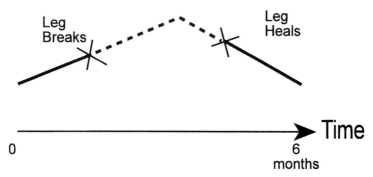

The dollar collapses in month 2 and the option is nearly worthless. However, the dollar recovers markedly in month 4 and the option rises in value

In times of currency volatility, it is quite possible to have a crippled spider that recovers. However, if the crippling of the spider were simply as a result of the purchase of the wrong contract, then a "secondary spider" may be created. This is a further spider superimposed upon the first spider, and it will necessarily have shorter legs because time will have elapsed. However, more money may need to be spent on the particular contract in question in order to right the wrongs of the leg underneath the secondary spider. Thus, the top spider will have "thicker legs". It is possible, therefore, to rescue the first spider by taking either opposite positions, reversing lines from black to white (or vice-versa), or by simply re-purchasing a contract at its new lower price in the hope of averaging out (An Egyptian Ratchet).

For example, imagine a contract is bought with a value of £1, but collapses to a value of 20p. The spider's leg is not yet broken, and so a secondary spider could go above it, purchase a great many more contracts at 20p, so that the average price of contracts purchased is, say, 33.3p. Therefore, a profit level will be reached on the two spiders when the contracts reach 33.3p and the deals can be closed out at no loss. In this way, a secondary spider can rescue an initial spider and, depending on the length of the leg and the colour of the lines, could rescue a crippled spider, or even a deaf spider.

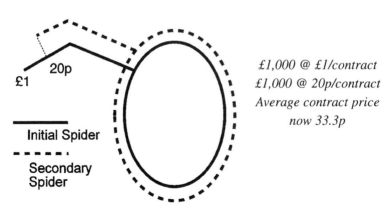

20p

£1

_____
Initial Spider

■ ■ ■ ■ ■
**Secondary
Spider**

£1,000 @ £1/contract
£1,000 @ 20p/contract
Average contract price
now 33.3p

Once a secondary spider has successfully rescued an initial spider, it is said that they have "mated".

Tarantula trading can be particularly effective in a market where there is some sort of artificial pegging between the currencies on the legs, such as the old ERM. By knowing the trading ranges, it is possible to predict the maximum movement between one currency and another because of the international central banks' need to support currencies that start to move outside the snake of the particular monetary union.

Such a system might allow a trade to construct a spider with effectively "unbreakable legs". That is to say that the options could not expire worthless because of the currency support operations that would occur in the market.

Sometimes, the initial spider can simply be a currency play; whilst the secondary, or tertiary spiders would be un-hedged interest rate contracts in the particular markets, so that there would be a dual element of risk involved, although interest rates and currencies are clearly linked.

Carousel Arbitrage

This is a very complex version of the spider. A carousel may have an unlimited number of legs, or limbs. In reality, however, the complexity of the carousel is actually limited by the market and the contracts that are available.

Imagine a carousel with eight horses on the outer ring and eight horses on the inner ring. Say that each outer horse represents a

Put option, and each inner horse represents a Call, or vice-versa. In this way, each pair of horses would, effectively, be a straddle.

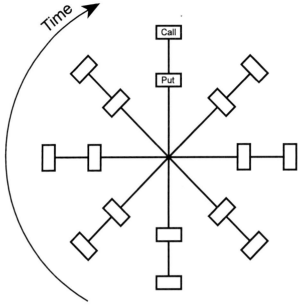

For example, if the outer horse were, say, a Futures contract written as a Put on the Nikkei Index, and each inner horse were a Future Call option on the Nikkei, then whenever the market rises, the value of the Call option rises and the Put option falls. At some point, therefore, as the carousel moves, (and its continual circular movement represents the elapse of time), the outer horse will rise as the inner horse falls and there will be a moment of equilibrium. At this point, an arbitrage opportunity will arise to close out the Call at a profit and re-purchase the Put at a value lower than that originally paid. If the market then recovers, as the carousel continues to spin, then the Put option value rises in a geared sense, and the gains can be spectacular.

So, if a Call option on the market began at 10p, and the Put option also began at 10p, the Call option might rise to 40p at which case it could be sold and the 40p invested in the Put option at, say, 5p. You now have nine times as many Put options contracts as previously, so that when the market recovers you should make many times the return on your original investment, which would otherwise have been the case.

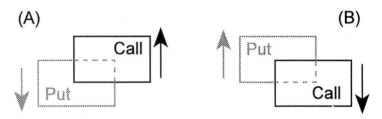

At position (A) the market has risen significantly. But at position (B) the market has fallen. The trader can close out the Put at a significant profit. He can then gear still further on a Call option by buying at the now vastly reduced price.

If a trader can successfully move from the outer horse to the inner horse at a moment of equilibrium, closing the outer deals at no loss, and gearing up his profits on the inner ring on every horse in question, then he will have "finessed the carousel". Whilst finessing the carousel may be a trader's ultimate goal, there are no known reported incidents of a successful finesse.

Egyptian Ratchet

Say you have unrealised profits on existing contracts. These will have the effect of decreasing your margin requirements. As an alternative, you can use these unrealised profits as margin to increase the size of your positions. You would do this in successive increments that would necessarily become smaller. A graphic representation of this takes the form of a pyramid, and this is known as an Egyptian Ratchet.

Alternatively, you might wish to benefit from falling prices. Pound cost averaging is a system whereby the repeated purchase of an asset, whose price is falling, results in the purchase of greater number of that asset at the successively lower prices.

Imagine, for example, that British Telecom shares begin to collapse. If you buy £1,000 worth at £4, and then £1,000 worth at £3, and then £1,000 worth at £2, you will see, as in the diagram below, that you build a pyramid of shares, and that the average price at which you can exit from the deal is £1.23.

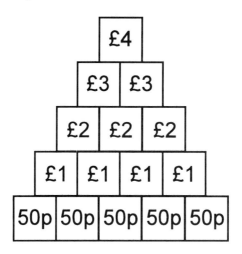

*Total holding of shares now 4,083 at a cost of £5,000
i.e. an average of £1.23*

If the share price starts to recover, and the trader believes that his original instinct that the price would exceed £4 will be realised, then he may continue to buy, thus constructing an inverted pyramid under the first pyramid and creating a Cape Fruit (so called because of the diamond shape).

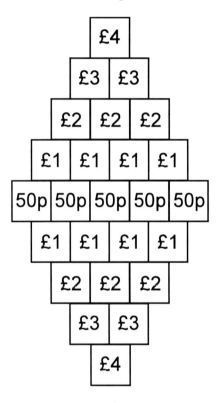

Total holding of shares rises to 6,166 at a cost of £9,000
i.e. an average of £1.46

As you will see, the trader now may exit at any time at a profit.

The Buy Write
(90-10 strategy)

This is a very sensible strategy for private investors. It involves the purchase of a stock as well as the purchase of an option on that stock or the writing of an option on that stock. Many leading experts consider this to be the safest and easiest strategy, some referring to it as free money.

For example, imagine that British Telecom shares are £9 each. You invest £900 in the shares, and at the same time you would invest the other £100 in a Call option, or a Put option, on those shares. What this means is that if the price collapses, you can exercise your Put option to make profits and then re-invest in the share at the collapsed price. If, alternatively, the price rises, you have the rise on the stock you bought and the geared rise on the option. Of course, if there is no major price movement then your option premium is lost.

Alternatively, you might invest your entire funds in British Telecom shares at £9, and then write an option on them. Imagine you write the option with an exercise price of £10, and you get an option premium of £1. If the share price rises, but not to £10, you will not be exercised. You will keep all the share price rise as well as the option premium. So, if the share price rise were 90p, in this example you will have almost doubled the growth on the shares. By whatever amount the share rises, the option premium will, effectively, be free money.

If the share price rises beyond your exercise price and you are exercised, then you have sold your shares at £10, and kept the option premium, making £2 on £9. If the expiration date of the option was, say three months out, then you should be entirely happy because you have made £2 on £9, i.e. 20%, in only three months.

This is an excellent strategy because, as long as you chose your exercise price as being the price at which you would have sold the shares in any event, then the option premium is always free money.

The Christmas Tree Spread

This involves the purchase of six options and the use of four strike prices. The method limits both risk and reward, but it does force a discipline on the trader, rather like a Spider or Carousel.
One Call is bought at the lower strike price, and the second strike price is ignored. Three Calls are sold at the third strike price, and two Calls are bought at the fourth strike price. This allows you a degree of price distribution (rather like a pools perm), and has the benefit of being relatively cheap.

The Butterfly Spread

This is a tactic, which involves four options, and three strike prices in an effort to limit risk. Whilst it also limits profit, this is nonetheless acceptable to many traders. The strategy would involve, for example, buying one Call at a low strike price, selling two Calls at the middle strike price, and buying one Call at the highest strike price. Alternatively, a Butterfly Put Spread would work by buying one Put at the highest strike price, selling two at the middle strike price, and buying one at the lowest strike price.

The Condor Spread

Once again, this is a trading strategy which can limit the downside potential, with an acceptable limit on the upside. The strategy works by buying one Call at a lower strike price, and selling one Call at the second strike price. A further Call is then sold at the third strike price and, finally, one Call bought at the fourth strike price. This strategy is often referred to as a Top Hat Spread.

Delta & Gamma

These are terms which refer to a hedging strategy to cover exposures in the Options and Futures market. Traders will calculate the likely change in the value of an Option based on a given change in the price of the underlying stock. The ratio of these two price movements is called the Delta and therefore expresses the likelihood of the Option value rising or falling based on rises or falls in the underlying price.

The Delta of an Option will usually be expressed as a value between zero and one. A Delta of 0.5 means that the Option would increase by around 0.5 units for each unit change in the value of the underlying stock (remember, the option costs less than the corresponding underlying stock, so the percentage gain or loss is larger).

For example, imagine you have written a Call Option of £10 million against the Swiss franc and have calculated the Delta at 0.7. The Option may rise or fall by £70,000 for each £100,000 rise or fall in the Exchange Rate between sterling and the Swiss franc.

This allows you to go out and purchase £7 million of Swiss francs in the spot market so that the value of this cash position should exactly offset the value of the Option written on sterling. This would then mean that the overall position would not be affected by changes in the Exchange Rate.

If the writer of an Option hedges by using such a cash position, he is said to be "Delta Neutral". Of course, these ratios will change as time goes by and frequent attention will be required in order to retain Delta Neutrality.

The Gamma may be defined as the change in the Delta for each change in the price of the underlying stock. In this way traders will use the Delta to balance their exposure, but as the Delta moves out will need to consider a Gamma in order to remain Delta Neutral overall. This is of particular importance when managing a very large book of diverse Option positions.

Cylinders

This system allows the purchaser to spend less in net terms on his option cover but at the same time the quid pro quo is that he loses part of the upside potential should markets move in his favour.

What happens is that the purchaser buys an Option but simultaneously writes an Option for the same amount but at a different strike price. This then allows him to offset the premium he has received for writing the Option against the cost of purchasing the first Option. The result is that the two payments are netted off and the smaller amount of cash has therefore to be spent.

Bostons

On occasions, the purchaser of an Option may not wish to actually expend the money. In this case a bank will provide a Boston, a means whereby the premium payment for the Option is deferred until the exercise date. Clearly, this will affect the profit involved because the bank will deduct the cost of the premium from the final proceeds, and at the same time factor in a cost for having effectively lent the Option premium to the purchaser.

Scouts

In the Foreign Exchange Market there can be a delay between the submission of a bid for an Option, and its successful award, or failed rejection. Because of competition, the average firm would not receive instructions on all the tenders it puts out.

Therefore, each Tenderer would necessarily need to carry open positions on far more contracts than it ever successfully receives. Scout stands for "Shares, Currency Option, Under Tender" and offers the Tenderers the chance to bid only in part to reduce the effect of being unsuccessful. This allows them to avoid an open ended FOREX commitment and provide full option cover at a fraction of the normal price, based on the number of Tenderers involved.

Caps

These allow borrowers to fix a level of interest rates over which they will not effectively be required to pay. Imagine for example, a large corporation has £100 million of loans at 10%. Clearly they need to pay £10 million per annum of interest.

If their gross profit for the year is £12 million, then they can pay this interest cost and still be left with a net profit of £2 million. However, if interest rates rise to 12% then there will be no net profit after interest costs, and at anything more than 12% the company will be running at a loss and heading for receivership.

By purchasing a "Ceiling Rate Agreement" the purchaser can Cap its exposure to interest rate rises.

The Floor

This hedges the opposite position to a Cap. Imagine for example, an institution is receiving interest payments on a floating basis and is therefore exposed to falling interest rates. It may construct Option contracts that effectively set a "Floor", so that if interest rates fall to that Floor, the options will be exercised and the profit will supplement the interest otherwise lost by falling rates.

Collars

A Collar is basically the combination of a Cap and a Floor where the purchaser is happy to limit the potential in either direction. What this means is that having purchased a Cap, a Floor is then written on some other term. This system allows a borrower to fix his interest rates between two set limits and therefore, a known range of interest rates differential.

Swaptions

It is possible for traders or hedgers to Swap interest rates with one another through the Swaps market, (see chapter three). However, sometimes borrowers and lenders will not wish to be committed in this fashion and would therefore like to take an Option to enter an interest rate Swap agreement. This is known as a Swaption because the buyer of that contract then has the option to enter into the Swap but not the obligation.

For example, imagine a large corporation can see that interest rates on a variable basis are currently rather low. However, they could rise at which point it might be too late to swap to a fixed rate loan to compensate for the effects of that rise. This is a dilemma. Should the corporation fix now and lose the benefit of the currently low variable rates, or go with the variable rate, thus being exposed to rising rates and missing the boat on the fixed rate. The answer is to buy a Swaption so that at a given time in the future the contract may be exercised and the loan effectively switched from variable to fixed.

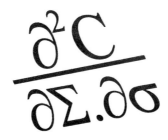

$$\frac{\partial^2 C}{\partial \Sigma . \partial \sigma}$$

Chapter Six

Risk

Derivatives trading is risky. You are faced with all the normal types of risk you would expect with a 'regular' investment, plus the gearing effect that derivatives bring. Let's look at these risks one by one.

Market Risk

Perhaps this is the most obvious form of risk involved in trading. It is impossible to predict the way whole markets will move. Sometimes a market may reflect bad news already so that when it actually happens, the market may rise rather than fall! This happened in 1989 when the Gulf War started and the major Stock Exchanges actually rose on the basis that the war would soon be over!

Specific Risk

Another obvious risk that is present in most forms of investment. It is the risk that your chosen stock will be subject to some form of bad news which doesn't affect similar stocks in the same market or sector.

Currencies

When trading any instrument you need to have a clearly defined exchange rate. For example it is pretty pointless if you are a UK trader and you write a contract in dollars only to see a rise in value cancelled out by a weakening of sterling against the dollar. You will need to hedge by buying a currency-based derivative contract!

Credit Risk

You have to be aware of the credit status of your counter-party. This is why a regulated exchange is such a useful facility. You must trade with your eyes open because there is the risk of counter-party default. Of course, in properly regulated and stable markets this is a rarity but, as chapter four shows, there are many occasions on which even the biggest, and most apparently solid, of institutions can over-reach themselves.

Liquidity Risk

This refers to the risk of a market being temporarily illiquid. Imagine the examples in earlier chapters when individuals or companies have taken an inappropriate position, or where a position becomes inappropriate. Clearly they will want to close it out or match it as quickly as possible. If a market is illiquid and nobody will trade with you, then you simply cannot do that. You could be left with a spiralling loss that is out of control. Once again, the existence of properly-regulated, liquid markets helps reduce the overall risk.

Earnings Risk

This is a very important risk, particularly for the sole trader. What we are trying to quantify is the effect on earnings of derivative trading activity. You might well make a profit on the contract itself. But you have to take into account other factors. For example, what has it actually cost you to run your business? You might well have an administrative assistant, you will have a colossal telephone bill, and you will undoubtedly have some sort of other administrative requirements. On top of this you will have a financing requirement, be it money you are borrowing with which to trade (I hope not), or the opportunity cost of using your own money which would otherwise be making you a basic rate of interest.

You must also factor in your time. I have met many sole traders who are delighted to "make" £50,000 a year trading. However, when you consider their financing costs, their technology costs, their premises and so on, whilst they are making £50,000 from the contracts they trade, their actual net profit is less than half that. When you consider that such individuals could probably earn more than the net amount by simply going to work each day then, despite their unblemished record of trading, they are actually losing money overall.

Valuation Risk

As you saw in Chapter One, the pricing of Traded Options is extremely complex. And you could correctly conclude that the pricing of more exotic derivatives is even more complex. So how do you work out if the price you are paying or receiving is correct? Even if you have a powerful computer to do the number crunching for you, there is a chance that you, or someone else might have entered an incorrect figure or variable at some point. What is more, there is no saying that the model you will be using is correct.

Legal Risk

This is a strange one, but terrifying for the sole trader or small company. Imagine your counterparty defaults on a trade. You go to law and recover your money, right? Not necessarily.

Under some jurisdictions a party could successfully argue that they were not actually authorised to have entered into the deal in the first place. If this is the case, then it may not be possible to force them to pay their losses.

Certain local government authorities in England have used this defence successfully. This is another reason why unsophisticated parties should be excluded from the market. They simply do not know what they are doing and they are sometimes not in a position to fulfil contracts or stand losses.

Regulation Risk

You have to be aware of the different regulatory procedures in different countries. Whilst there is an attempt to harmonise between major markets, there are enormous cultural and practical differences in doing this. The level of regulation and the degree of its enforcement will therefore be different. If you suddenly find yourself making marvellous profits very easily in a less than mainstream market, then you need to beware.

Ratings Risk

There are several independent bodies, such as Standard and Poors, who produce credit ratings for institutions. Of course, one has to rely on the full report rather than just the Triple A rating or whatever. This is because an organisation may have considerable positions within its portfolio which are yielding profits. These profits feed through to a reduced requirement for loan finance and would therefore give the organisation an apparently stronger balance sheet. Accordingly, two apparently-identical banks could have very different derivative exposure. You will need to discover this for yourself and it is all part of the research aspect of your trading.

Personal Risk

If you are a major institution, then you can normally stand an embarrassing derivative scandal however expensive. Sometimes it may be massive such as Barings, or Sumitomo, to the effect that an organisation might actually be wiped out. But generally speaking big institutions can cope.

Of course, this does not apply to sole trading individuals and small companies. There is the very serious risk of personal bankruptcy and all the psychological and practical effects this would have on the trader's family, friends and in some sad cases, health. You must go into this market with your eyes wide open, with all the information you need (much more than is in this book), in order to limit the effects of things going wrong.

You should talk to a competent lawyer and financial adviser. It may be prudent to move assets into the name of your spouse or other family members so that you know exactly how much it is you are risking. If you are not prepared to face the worst, then you really should not become involved in derivatives trading, apart from perhaps the simple purchase of contracts in fairly regulated markets and with underlying such as shares or something else which is particularly comprehensible to you.

More forms of risk are covered in the '*International Dictionary of Derivatives*' by Alex Kiam, also published by TTL.

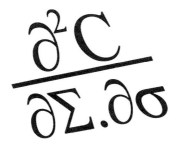

$$\frac{\partial^2 C}{\partial \Sigma . \partial \sigma}$$

Chapter Seven

Case Studies

Here are a few fictitious examples of derivatives in action. They illustrate a variety of circumstances from where positions may need to be hedged to situations where a trader may see a profit opportunity.

The Large International Company Treasurer

These days, for a great many organisations the world is one big market. However, this creates not simply problems of differing trade practices and cultures, but those surrounding the currency in which an organisation is paid for the work it does, because it may have to pay for that work in a different currency. So, in addition to all the other balancing acts that the Treasurer has to carry out, matching loans with liabilities, managing overnight positions and the like, the hedging of currency takes on major importance.

For example, imagine an international car company based in the U.K. receives an order for 500 motorcars at $20,000 each, to be delivered in 12 months time. At first the board of the company rejoice at the idea of a $10 million order, but the prudent Treasurer points out the risks that such an order could in fact make the company go bankrupt!

Say at the time of striking the deal that the exchange rate is $1.20 to the £1. This means that the order is worth £8.33 million, or £16,666 per car. The company calculate that each car costs £12,000 to manufacture and deliver, so there is a healthy profit.

A year down the line however, the dollar has weakened considerably and there are now $2 to every £1. If so, once the $10 million is paid and converted to sterling it would be worth only £5 million (just £10,000 per car).

Not only have they lost the profit they expected to make on the cars, but they have also made a loss of £2000 on each car. So the swing in exchange rates has effectively lost the manufacturing company £3.33 million. Clearly, a loss of that magnitude is enough to make even well-capitalised organisations go out of business.

Thankfully, the prudent Treasurer has the answer. He buys a currency option over the 12 months on $10 million at an agreed rate of $1.20 to the £1. A year later when the dollar has weakened to $2 to the £1, he simply receives the $10 million and instead of converting them into only £5 million, he converts them into £8.33 million as planned. The work has been profitable and the company is saved.

Of course, the currency may go the other way. For example, if the dollar had strengthened so that there was $1 to the £1, then the company would have taken back the $10 million due on delivery and converted them into sterling, making an extra £1.66 million over and above their expected profit.

Some major organisations have such a complex mix of assets and liabilities that they might be able to handle temporary swings between currencies. But as many organisations work on much finer profit margins than are used in this example, even small currency movements can be enough to make a particular piece of work unattractive. Viewed against this major risk, the price of a currency option is highly attractive. In practice a company of this nature would probably have the extra cost built into its margins when pricing the product in the first place.

Interest Rate Swaps

Imagine two large corporations need to borrow the same amount of money over the same period. The one corporation is triple-A rated and can therefore borrow at a fixed rate of 9% or a floating rate of Libor plus two, say, 12%.

The other, or second, borrower has a poorer credit rating and therefore the fixed interest rate it can achieve is 11%, but the floating rate would be Libor.

Because the differential between the rate at which the "less-sound" borrower and the rate at which the triple-A rated borrower could pay for funds is greater than the differential between the rate at which the "less-good" borrower and the triple-A borrower would pay for floating rate funds, they have the opportunity to effect a swap.

The second borrower therefore borrows at Libor and the triple-A company borrows at 9% fixed. They enter into a swap agreement and the second borrower agrees to pay an additional ½% premium to the triple-A rated institution.

This produces a total interest cost to the second borrower of 9½%. If this party's borrowing would otherwise have cost more than 9½% (as in this example), then it benefits from the swap.

The stronger borrower also benefits because it receives the ½% premium and its floating rate funds are therefore reduced by that amount, thus dropping its borrowing cost to Libor minus ½%.

Each party must then pay the differential between the two interest rates once all the terms have been agreed and set.

The Professional Fund Manager

Imagine the dilemma of the professional fund manager. It is a very competitive world, and he has to produce results to keep the money flowing into the organisation for which he works and in order to keep his job. This leaves him open to the problem that his competitors might use derivative strategies in order to improve their performance, so that if he does not take the same steps, he might fall behind.

In the long term, he might produce a more consistent performance, but so much in the investment world is now based on short-term results that he may be forced to take positions.

Moreover, most fund managers fail to beat the market in which they invest; even if they invest in the index itself, their dealing costs, and time lag in copying the index perfectly, will necessarily mean that they under-perform.

Imagine, therefore, a fund manager who is holding all the stocks in the FT Index and has a fund overall worth many millions of pounds. He might decide to take the dividend yield, which is usually between, say, 4% and 6% gross on the FT Index, and spend that money on Index Futures or Options.

He might buy a Call Option so that if the index were to rise considerably, he could close out the option at a large profit and thereby boost the performance of his fund. This would give him the prospects of slight out-performance, but, when judged against the context that he might not be able to out-perform at all otherwise, it is quite attractive.

Alternatively, he might buy a Put Option. If the market were to take a fall, he could exercise or sell his option at a very large profit and therefore have protected his fund against that fall. This again would be out-performance against the index.

By adopting this strategy, it might be possible for the fund manager to out-perform in both a rising and a falling market. The problem, however, is that in a static market, he would under-perform. Without the volatility, neither the Put nor the Call option would be valuable, and he would have lost his dividend stream by using it to pay option premiums. This strategy would therefore work in times of volatility, such as in the run-up to an election, in places where the market is inherently volatile, for example, the Far East, or in volatile sectors such as TMTs.

The Second Professional Fund Manager

Jealous of the first fund manager's ability to outperform the market, this fund manager discovers that options are behind the success of his colleagues. He decides, therefore, to write option contracts in the belief that his portfolio and the market are not going to rise, that he will not be exercised, and will therefore be able to keep the option premium as extra income for the fund.

Imagine, therefore, in the first quarter of the year, that he writes a Put option, and the market rises. Because he will not be exercised, he takes the option premium and has out-performed the market. In the subsequent quarter, he writes a Call option and the market falls back to where it was at the beginning of the period. He has now received two option premiums and his fund is seen to be out-performing.

In the next quarter he again writes a Call option, but this time the market rises considerably and, as the option expiry date approaches, he either waits to be exercised or writes a Put option to gain more money, or closes out his position by buying a stock index future. Now he has lost all the extra money that he has made in the first two quarters and he is beginning to under-perform. In the final quarter, therefore, he takes double options or a straddle, believing that the market will not move outside the trading range that has been established.

However, the market has an enormous Bull Run at which point he has to sell stock in order to meet his margin obligations. Then, the market corrects itself and goes through the bottom end of his trading range. Now he is exercised by the Put option holders and, similarly, has to buy stock from them as per the agreement. He has now destroyed the performance of his fund and, at the end of the year, is at the bottom of the performance table.

The mistake he has made is that of failing to understand the risk. The first fund manager simply bought Put and Call options and could never lose any more than his option premiums. At any time he could sell his option in the market and peg his loss at a set figure. The second fund manager, however, was writing options, and this meant that his losses were geared well beyond the amount of premium he laid down.

The Emigrant

Imagine a successful businessman who is appointed to a US company at a senior level. He will be required to work there for at least five years and decides to move his family and educate his children in the United States. The problem he faces is that of his position on return to the UK. Imagine for example, that he owns a house worth £500,000 in London, and that the exchange rate with the dollar is at one for one.

By selling the house he can then take his $500,000 to the United States and either buy a property there or invest the money. Five years later however on his return, the exchange rate could have moved to, say, two dollars to the pound, so that his $500,000 now only buys £250,000, and hence a property which is half the size of that which he previously owned.

To compound the problem, imagine there is another UK housing boom in the five-year period. In this case, houses have doubled in sterling terms so that his former home now costs £1,000,000 and he could buy only a quarter of it!

Many people fear being left out of the UK housing market during another rise such as took place during the 1980s. This leads them to retain their house in the UK and rent it out with all the attendant problems of administration and maintenance. Additionally, any income from rental may be taxable, and, depending on the number of years spent renting the house, there can be capital gains tax complications.

Further, by not selling the UK home, there will be no free cash to buy a home in the United States, which will either mean a very considerable mortgage, or high rates of rental. The whole exercise is complex.

Fortunately, the individual in question understands the derivatives market and takes two basic strategies. He writes a property option, and he locks into the dollar rate forward.

The property option is not something that can be traded on a recognised exchange and so he has to create a bespoke option with a willing third party. He approaches the owner of a home that he would like to live in five years hence, and it is valued at £500,000. He pays that owner £10,000 for the option to buy the house for £500,000 at any time in the next five years.

If the market rises to £1,000,000, as in this example, then his £10,000 option will be very valuable, and he will exercise it buying the house at the current level of £500,000 and not the future inflated level. (Incidentally, the option writer believes that property will not rise and is simply making £10,000 for doing nothing in the meantime. Either party could of course be right.)

The second transaction for our emigrant is that of selling the dollar forward. He keeps his sale proceeds from his own home in sterling and sells the dollar whilst it is one for one. When in five years hence it is two for one, he could close out the contract at a cost of only £250,000 so that he has, in effect, doubled his money.

Of course, this example is simple and contrived, but, nonetheless, the principle holds good. By using a derivative contract, or a variety of derivative contracts, an ordinary individual may protect himself against movements in currencies, markets or interest rates that would have had an adverse effect on his planning.

The Small Expanding Company

Imagine a company which has been slowly, but surely, building its business and moving from one league to another in terms of the type of work it can take on. Because of its growing reputation for quality and reliability, it is offered a major contract, which will double its turnover. The finance director calculates that of the £10M turnover brought in by this contract, £1M will become net profit. Whilst the Board of the company are delighted and all the employees can see stability in winning such a contract, the FD has to point out the problems.

Clearly, in order to finance such expansion and the extra contract, money will have to be borrowed. At the current rate of, say, 3% over base, this equates to a 10% interest rate. The FD calculates that the company would remain in profit so long as interest rates did not rise by more than three points. If they do, then the profit on the job goes, and, given the size of the increase in turnover, the company could become seriously illiquid, and even go out of business.

A fixed rate is suggested so that a degree of certainty can be introduced to the planning. But for a company of this size, a fixed rate costs 2% more than the current floating rate and there will then be no profit in the job at all. Moreover, over the period of doing the job, it is forecast that rates might fall, and the benefit of this would be lost by taking a fixed rate. The Board face a dilemma - they either take the risk that rates will rise during the period of the job and force them out of business, or take a fixed rate in which there is no profit, simply turnover and prestige. The scope for disaster if something else goes wrong in the manufacturing or delivery process means that they cannot take the latter position.

They decide on the following strategy. First of all they borrow all the money on a floating rate and immediately put it on deposit, only using the money to pay suppliers at the last moment during the period of the contract. This means that they will have deposit interest to offset, in part, against the cost of borrowing. However, they fix a Floor on their deposit rate by buying the appropriate Futures contract. What this means is that if interest rates fall, then they will continue to receive the current level of interest on their cash deposit. In times of extreme volatility, they could find that they are making more on deposit than they are actually paying out in interest costs.

At the same time, they buy a Cap so that if interest rates rise to 12%, they will receive extra income from the market to offset the costs of servicing the loan.

They are now protected in that falling rates will result in a decreasing differential between the deposit rate and the borrowing rate, whilst rising rates would result in the Cap operating on the borrowing, and their deposit rate would rise to provide extra income and profit in the whole equation. Whilst the contracts will cost money, they will only be a fraction of the turnover in question, and a very useful insurance policy.

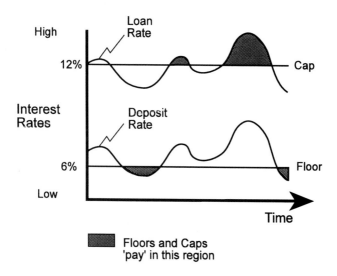

The Retiring Businessman

Imagine the owner of a small family company has traded successfully from purpose built premises offering chilled distribution. He therefore has a very particular type of building that will be of little use to most people, who would have to remove all the expensive chilling equipment. However, another firm in the same business would be most attracted to an already-built and equipped site. This could be an International organisation with little coverage in his area.

The problem that the individual faces is that he cannot actually retire for another nine months for tax reasons and that he does not wish to dispose of the building and crystallise any capital gain in this trading period. Additionally, the purchaser may be a foreign owned concern that does not wish to enter into the contract until their next trading period so that their accounts for this trading period show a particular complexion.

If the contract were struck today, but with delayed completion, this would not suit either party - the date of the striking of the contract would be the important one for a high-rate tax payer, and the contingent liability of buying the building might need to be reported in the overseas company's consolidated accounts.

The fear, which both parties have, is that currency could go against them. For example, imagine the property is worth £1M, and that equates to three million Deutsch Marks. If the pound strengthens, then the international group will have to find more Deutsch Marks. Alternatively, if the pound were to weaken, then the UK individual would receive fewer Deutsch Marks, if the contract were 'DM denominated'.

In this example, each party would hedge their position by dealing in a foreign exchange forward contract in the appropriate currency to fix the rate. For the individual, this would give him the certainty of receiving £1M, which will set him up for retirement. The international corporation, however, might take a more pro-active view and might decide to take a "participating break forward", or a simple break-forward, so that if the currency goes against them, they are protected, but if things go in their favour, they can break the contract and reap at least some of the upward potential.

Once again, the derivatives market provides the answer to an otherwise worrying problem.

The Trader/Market Punter

A lot of people have views on the Stock Market, or on particular shares, but are unable to make any real money. For example, imagine that a stock market punter is a great meteorologist and believes that we are to have the longest, hottest summer ever. He thinks that shares in Cadbury Schweppes and Guinness will both rise as a result of this. However, on doing his homework, he discovers that there will be no more than, say, a 10% or 15% rise over the six months of long hot summer.

Given that other factors might depress the market by an equivalent amount and neutralise such a gain, he is reluctant to invest. He calculates that the gain he can guarantee to make is no more than 5%, and so to make any real money in absolute terms, he would have to invest hundreds of thousands of pounds, which he simply does not have.

The answer is for him to buy a Call option on both stocks that would expire in September of the year in question. If the option were to cost, say, 20 pence when the share price is £4, then when the share price rises to £4.50, the option price could be worth 50 pence, (assuming the exercise price for the shares was £4). In this example, therefore, he has made 150% even though the share has risen by only 12.5%. Instead of turning £40,000 into £45,000 as he would have done as a shareholder, he could turn £40,000 into £100,000 by the gearing effect of options.

Encouraged by his profit, he decides to continue playing the market. He believes that it will fall, and so he buys a Put option on the FTSE index.

Due to the political problems he predicted, the market falls dramatically and he is able to close out his option position at a massive profit. He now reasons that the market must bounce back and so rolls-over all his profit and original stake into a Call option. During the life of the option the market does improve considerably and his profit is magnified once again. In a period of months he has made several hundred percent, and he decides to order a new Ferrari.

He now thinks of himself as king of the option market and decides to write options because he knows his judgement is right more often than it is wrong. He therefore writes a Call option, believing that the market will not rise. It doesn't, and he keeps the option premium. He then repeats this across all stocks in the FTSE index, and as none of them rise appreciably, he once again retains the option premiums.

Then he makes his mistakes. He identifies a penny share that he thinks is likely to go bust. It is currently priced at 10 pence and he writes Call options against it. However, over the next few weeks it is heavily written up in the penny share guides and the weekend press, with the result that the price rises and rises and rises. The exercise price remains at 10 pence, but the share price goes to £1. Given all the interest in the stock, a major competitor now feels that they have to buy them out and makes an offer of £2 a share.

At this point, all option holders exercise their options to buy at 10 pence and our punter is forced to go in the market buying at £2 and selling at 10 pence. He has lost £1.90 for every option he wrote. That is to say, he has made a 1,900% loss on his option position, and is forced to cancel his order for his Ferrari, sell his Ford and his home!

The message is clear. Don't let a short period of successful trading allow you to move outside your limits or to believe that you are invincible. Secondly, never write uncovered options. If you must write options, make sure you have the stock to deliver so that you know precisely what your maximum loss can be.

Investment Group

An investment group carries out all its market research to see what individual investors want. It discovers that what individuals want is the safety of a Building Society account, but the returns of the Stock Market. They want to keep their cake and eat it. They understand that there is more money to be made in the Stock Market than they will ever make in the Building Society, but they also understand that it is a complex market staffed by professionals where the pitfalls are many and the potential losses are great. As a result, billions of pounds remain in UK Building Societies doing very little for the owners of those accounts.

But the institution has the answer. It designs a product which will guarantee to return the investor's money intact at the end of three years, or provide 100% of the rise in the FT index for that period if greater. So the punters now have the option to participate in the Stock Market on the upside, and yet guarantee that they will never lose any money. The product is massively successful and immediately oversubscribed.

The managers now have to construct the product along the lines of the model they previously created. The first thing they might do is to take 82% of each investors' money and buy a certificate of deposit (CD) with an interest rate which is approximately 7% a year fixed for the three year period. This means that the 82% will grow back to 100% as promised.

This leaves them with 18% with which to play. (The reality is that they would probably snaffle 10% as a charge, but for the purposes of this example, we will assume it is 18!) With this unallocated fund, therefore, they can buy a Stock Index Future geared to equal the market's rise three years hence. Imagine, therefore, the UK market were to rise 40% over that period, then they would need to find £4,000 for every £10,000 which the investor placed with them. As they have only £1,800 with which to achieve that £10,000, they need a return of 5.5 times their original stake, notwithstanding that the CD will mature anyway. They would buy a Call option or a variety of Futures contracts geared for three years hence. The book of contracts would be constructed in such a way that whatever the rise the market might be, there would be a contract, or range of contracts capable of producing the necessary gearing as promised.

In fact, the market has become very sophisticated and there is now a wide range of options available. For example, it is now possible to lock into any degree of capital guarantee from 70% to 150%. Moreover, your participation rate in the upside of the market can be anything from 25% to 350%. (Sadly, you cannot have 150% capital guarantee and 350% market participation!)

One of the most exciting institutional products for private investors is the quarterly ratchet system.

Imagine, for example, that the UK Stock Market rises by 10% in the first quarter, falls by 20% in the second quarter, rises by 20% in the third quarter and then a further 10% in the final quarter. Assuming £10,000 were invested, ignoring all charges, then at the end of the first quarter the £10,000 would be worth £11,000. At the end of the second quarter, it would have fallen to £8,800, rising to £10,560 at the end of third quarter. On the first anniversary it would have reached £11,616. You would therefore have made 16% at a time when the market's annual rise was in fact 20%!

Now compare this with the geared system which gives you a capital guarantee of 85%, and an upside of 300%. In the first quarter, your £10,000 grows to £13,000. In the second quarter it falls to only £11,050, rising to £17,680 at the end of the third quarter. It then reaches £22,984 at the end of the year. You have made 129% at a time when the market grows by only 20%, and when your conventional investing colleagues made only 16%.

This is the power of gearing, and if you were to go back through time and reconstruct products based on the actual movements in the Stock Market, you would find that for the ten years between 1984 and 1994 a sum of £10,000 would have returned a figure of £600,000!

The US Citizen

Imagine a man is the chief executive of a U.S. Corporation working in the U.K. He has been working for 10 years and put down roots, buying a home and having various investments. He is paid in sterling and all his liabilities are denominated in sterling.

He has been very successful and is due to retire in 12 months time. Despite having enjoyed his time in the U.K. he still considers himself an American and would like to return there to retire.

The problem he faces is that converting his U.K assets of £1M into $1.5M will allow him to live comfortably in retirement in the United States, buying a home and creating an investment portfolio. However, he remembers a friend of his whose assets were sufficient for the rest of his life when the dollar was two to the pound, but who was forced to retire when the dollar was one to the pound and therefore could not afford to settle in the United States.

He faced the Hobson's choice of being forced to either convert at the unfavourable exchange rate, and take the consequences, or to wait until such time as the unpredictable exchange rate might improve. Clearly, the latter is very inconvenient, whilst the former is probably unacceptable.

So, our U.S. citizen decides to hedge his bets and buy a forward contract in the Forex market to convert his £1M sterling to $1.5M in 12 months. He can then be certain that unless there is raging inflation in the U.S. he should be able to achieve his aims. In many ways, this type of hedging is like an insurance policy - the money is dead money if the contingent event doesn't arise, but of course, if it does, the money spent on the derivative contract has been worth every penny.

However, as chief executive of an international organisation, our citizen is something of a punter, and decides also to construct his contract as a break-forward. This means that if the dollar goes in his favour, he will still be able to participate in that, and may even improve his position. Imagine, for example, that the dollar moves to $1.75 to the pound, he would be able to benefit from this and, in fact, retire to the States slightly wealthier than he had calculated his needs.

The Stock Broking Firm

A small firm of stockbrokers has been selected to bring a new company to the market. Whenever this happens there will suddenly be a large proportion of stock available which was previously held by private individuals, institutions or banks. If all the stock which is issued is immediately snapped up by the market, as it has been in Government privatisation for example, then there is no problem.

However, in some cases, the stock is simply not attractive and isn't all purchased. Even when the stock is attractive, the market might crash during the offer period so that the stock which was coming to the market at 50 pence per share, and considered to be reasonably valued, might now be worth only 30 pence. Unfortunately, the offer price has been fixed and there is no way of altering it.

Stockbrokers are often asked to underwrite the issue. That is to say that if the issue is not a success and all the stock is not bought, then they will have to buy it themselves and take the loss. Of course, there is an underwriting premium for this activity. If the issue is a success, then the underwriting premium is simply more profit. If the issue is a failure however, then the underwriting profits are unlikely to be able to match the loss on the stock.

As one of the major reasons for issues flopping is that the market changes significantly between the beginning of the offer and the actual floatation, it would be possible for the stockbrokers to take their profit from the underwriting and buy a Stock Index Future in the U.K. market. Accordingly, if the market fell dramatically, there would be profit from the Futures contract which would help offset the underwriting loss. For a small stockbroker, which might not be heavily capitalised, this could be the only option to cover their position.

Chapter Eight

When It All Goes Wrong

A little knowledge is a dangerous thing, and the highly complex area of derivatives should not be approached without extreme caution and a thorough understanding of the risks involved. Over the years, there have been many high profile examples of individuals and organisations who have used derivatives instruments with some success and gradually become more relaxed about the risks. This had led them to take bigger and bigger positions, and to sometimes take positions for their own sake. Rather than just utilising the particular instrument that will suit a specific position, individuals and corporations have crossed the fine line between exploiting these instruments, and simply trading in them for speculative gains.

There is a common thread that runs through all the various scandals and disasters outlined in this section. That individual traders or corporations began by using derivatives sensibly. They bought or sold contracts they understood and, generally, understood the exposure. After initial successes they moved on, perhaps buying contracts that they did not understand, and gearing up for risks that were simply not appropriate.

There are those who think that one day there will be a derivative trading scandal where the losses are so great, and the gearing so enormous, that very few parties involved will be able to meet their obligations and there will be a world-wide financial systems collapse. Read on, and see how it is likely to happen.

A 'Textbook' Example

During the bullish Stockmarket of 1986 and 1987 it seemed everyone could make money. The simple purchase of a new issue stock, or a blue chip share usually meant profit. It was even possible to buy one of the many penny shares and wonder stocks that would make quite fantastic gains. Of course, in a market like that, the gearing effect of traded options is absolutely phenomenal. A share that doubles and doubles again can make the option holder several hundred times his original stake money. Against this background fortunes were made, and sadly, lost.

An 'A'-Level Student had studied and spotted the attractions of Options. He dealt through a major bank, at first, simply buying put and call Options and trading them whenever there was price volatility. He always met his margin requirements and owing to a degree of judgement and a rising market made more and more money. This, of course, led the bank to allow him to trade in more and more contracts and ever-larger amounts.

Unfortunately, the majority of his trading was one way, so that he required continually rising markets. In addition to this, he began to write Options rather than simply buy them. Worse still, he wrote uncovered Options. That is to say, that he wrote Options on Stock that he didn't have. Then came the crash of October 1987

- Black Monday, as it became known. The other parties to his Option transaction then exercised him in the belief that he would be able to buy stock from them at pre-crash levels. Of course, in order to do so he would have had to find many hundreds of thousands of pounds, which being even a prudent and skilful trader, a schoolboy may find hard to do. Of course, when the truth eventually came to light it was clear that the bank had been rather lax in allowing him to build up the positions in the first place, and was forced to pay compensation from their errors and omissions account so that the holders of the Option contracts could have them fulfilled.

The writer of a book on derivatives could not wish for a better salutary tale on how Options can catch out the unwary investor. If this were the only scandal of its kind it would still be worthy of discussion for years thereafter. Unfortunately, there are those who never learn and the rest of this section is devoted to considering some of the more dramatic failures which have resulted not in thousands of pounds being lost, but millions, tens of millions and hundreds of millions.

The Colombo Scandal

Marc Colombo was a Foreign Exchange Dealer in his late twenties working for the Zurich branch of a major bank. He had been recruited to establish the Foreign Exchange Department and make profits on the various arbitrage opportunities, which existed for such a bank, along with more ordinary capital market ventures.

He made good profits for the bank in the early days of his appointment, taking positions inside the limits which had been set for his activities. However, in late 1974, Colombo sold forward $34 million because he believed that the dollar was about to fall. His idea was that he would subsequently buy back the dollars at the lower price, close out the deal, and make a considerable profit.

The problem that Colombo faced was that the dollar didn't fall. In fact, due to the oil crisis the dollar was seen as a popular haven for international capital, and as a result of supply and demand, it rose significantly.

Colombo now faced a dilemma. To close out the deal now would simply mean taking a loss. And that loss would have been very significant within the limits of his activities. As an alternative, he bought sufficient dollars to balance his forward position, in case the dollar continued to rise. This left him with a position where he had lost millions but instead of reporting this to his employers, he hoped that matters might eventually right themselves and that he could buy time in which to sort the problems out. He therefore bought $100 million forward, gambling that the dollar would go higher still. At the same time, he sold the dollar forward again, this time for $600 million, in case the dollar fell. It didn't, and his losses now totalled over £30 million sterling.

When the banking authorities received a tip-off based on Colombo's unusually large transactions, they discovered that he had open positions, that is to say those which are not covered by a contrary compensating contract, of over $500 million dollars. This was more than a hundred times the open position limit that Colombo had been set by his employers!

Ironically, if Colombo had made no further deals and had been allowed to carry the positions through to maturity, the losses would have been much smaller, and might even have turned into a profit. This is what motivates and excites the Foreign Exchange dealer and sometimes tempts him to move outside his dealing limits. At any moment a wild movement in a currency can suddenly turn a desperate loss-making situation into an heroic profit.

Instead Colombo was jailed on charges of forgery and false accounting, leaving behind him a massive embarrassment that shook the confidence of the Zurich and international financial communities.

Making the Pips Squeak
Orange County

Orange County in America is just to the south of Los Angeles in sunny California. It was caused to file for bankruptcy after the county's treasurer, Mr Robert Citron, made public the information that the county's investment funds had been severely hit by a loss of $1.5 Billion!

The Orange County investment pool was the fund into which all the County's tax receipts were invested. In the early 1990s the fund managers had a great deal of success. They out-performed other fixed interest funds very considerably, and the pool grew with more and more money being deposited. Having made the interest rate prediction correctly, and therefore being successful, the manager continued to gamble.

His problem arose from the derivative contract he used, known as "inverse floaters". This is a kind of loan, which is linked to Libor. However, if Libor goes down, then the rates on these floaters go up. Of course, if Libor goes up, then the rates on the notes go down. At the same time of course, the capital value of those notes will decline because the coupon has declined so markedly.

Having, therefore, damaged the value of the portfolio, the manager decided that he was right about declining interest rates, and wanted to invest more. In order to be able to invest more, he had to borrow. In fact, over $12 Billion was borrowed, further increasing the gearing and the ratchet effect of the rates going the wrong way. Because in 1994, Libor went from 3.6 to 6.8%, those institutions and brokers who had lent to the fund manager required further collateral to cover their position. Unfortunately, the fund didn't have it, and filed for bankruptcy.

What is most significant about this particular situation, is that the public funds effectively deposited by ordinary people were the subject of a derivative trading strategy which very few of them knew about, and still fewer understood. How would you feel if your county or state was speculating with your money to the point of bankruptcy? Who would then fund local government, education and services? Whilst standards of this nature may be an occupational hazard for major financial institutions, that local government could be involved has sent shock waves through the derivatives industry.

The Man Who Broke the Bank

The most dramatic of all the various scandals involving derivatives is surely that of Barings Bank and its rogue trader Nick Leeson. The losses were accumulated on a scale previously unknown, and Mr Leeson's subsequent disappearance with accusations of the bank having been brought down by a conspiracy of Far Eastern businessmen, added to the bizarre aspect of the fiasco.

Barings Bank was one of the best names in the City of London. A blue-blooded bank whose history went back to the 18th Century, and whose charitable works through the Baring Foundation were the envy and admiration of many. Years ago, the bank had been considered to be one of the great powers in the world controlling such a large proportion of the world's finance that they were able to fund Government activities, and contribute greatly to the development of trade and the Industrial Revolution. With such a reputation, and still largely in private hands, many thought they were invincible.

Nick Leeson was a 28 year old trader from Watford, England. He had left school after having failed 'A' level Maths, and went into the City. At first, his responsibilities were relatively minor support roles in the settlement system. Whenever a deal is transacted, there is a significant electronic or paper-trail behind it which needs to be managed. This is known as the "back office". Leeson's experience was as a settlements clerk in the Barings back office.

However, like many support staff in the City, Leeson had ambitions. He saw himself as a glamorous trader in the markets, and when the opportunity to go to Singapore came, Leeson took it.

Once in Singapore, Leeson worked as a clerk at Simex, the Singapore International Monetary Exchange. He was generally thought to be good at his job and was therefore given increased responsibility. Based on this experience, Barings managed to get Leeson a trading licence. Over the ensuing months, Leeson was recognised as a very talented and skilled trader. By 1993, he was the general manager for Barings Futures in Singapore.

As time went by, Barings Singapore became increasingly successful. In a mere seven months to July 1994, the Singapore trading activities provided a profit of $30M - almost 20% of the entire Barings' Group profit for the whole of the previous year.

But there were those that had their doubts. Some saw Barings' activities as the well-controlled visions of a bank with exceptional staff - leaders in their field. Others saw Barings' growing confidence as dangerous, and began to be at first amazed, and then alarmed, by the size of the positions they took.

Barings had several major strategies based on the two most important Simex Futures contracts. These were based on the Nikkei 225 Stock Market Index, and the Japanese Government Bond future. Over the years, the trading in these contracts had moved away from Tokyo to Osaka in the South of Japan, and also to Singapore. This allowed identical contracts to be traded in the three different centres at different prices based on market conditions and currency exchange. Even though the difference in prices was tiny, it would, nonetheless, be significant if dealing frequently and in large volumes. The five strategies that Barings employed were as follows:

Inter Exchange Arbitrage

Under this system, contracts would be purchased or sold in both Singapore and Tokyo, or Osaka. All the contracts would be matched so that no open positions were left, and the profit would simply be made on the arbitrage between the fractional price movements. As members of both the Osaka and the Singapore Exchanges, Barings were able to access information on both markets simultaneously.

Taking positions

When an organisation is as powerful as Barings, it will know what other market traders are doing. It will be able to use its immense capital to squeeze out the smaller traders who may be forced to sell at a loss, because they just don't have the money to hold open positions overnight.

Spread Price Differentials

This allowed Barings to make money on the difference between the prices quoted for "spreads", i.e. several contracts expiring on different dates, and prices quoted for the individual contracts in each different market.

Liquidity Arbitrage

There is greater liquidity in the Osaka Derivatives market than in Singapore. So, given the amount of trades, which Barings was affecting, it could allow its clients to combine the better prices from Singapore with the greater liquidity from Osaka.

Large Order Arbitrage

Market knowledge would tell Barings of a large unfulfilled order in one market. This would then allow them to build up their own position in another market. During the day, as news of the large order in the other market became public, the price would move as a result of sentiment, thus allowing Barings to close out their smaller deal at a profit.

It is clear that, in the early days, Barings were carrying out these trades very successfully, but in January 1995, it appears that somebody in the bank introduced a new trading strategy. They started to sell Put and Call options on the Nikkei 225 Index, receiving the premium for writing those options, and allegedly putting the proceeds into an unauthorised trading account, numbered 88888 - significant to the superstitious local community.

By writing both Put and Call options, struck at the same exercise price, Barings was creating a "straddle". This is a bet on stability in the market, that it will not rise significantly nor fall significantly. As long as the market remains within the trading range of the straddle, the bank pockets the profits on the option premiums and is never exercised.

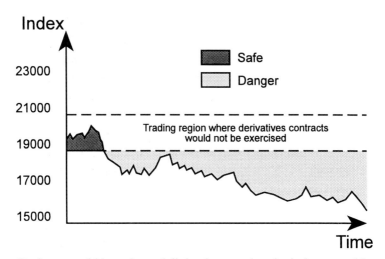

Barings would have been delighted to see that the index stayed in the narrow range between 19,000 and 21,000 points. Against this background they continued to make a profit.

The bank apparently also expected a New Year rally, which often happens in Stock Markets, but this failed to materialise. As a result, the index fell to the lower end of Barings' expected trading range. But they were still ahead.

However, in the early hours of January 17th, an enormous earthquake hit Japan's industrial centres of Kobe and Osaka. This was one of the largest earthquakes for years, and was bound to affect the market. At first the market fell down to around 19,000, namely the bottom end of Barings' safe trading range. However, matters got worse. On Monday 23rd January, the Nikkei 225 dropped down to 17,950 points. Barings faced a dilemma. They were now well out-of-the-money and began heavy buying of March and June 1995 Futures contracts.

The pressure was on and Barings had to cover their position. The bank was about to make a massive bet that things would improve and they would come out ahead once again as king of the traders. However, the market slid further, down to 17,605 points, and this left Barings with an estimated loss of some £380M. One of the theories was that Barings, or someone within the bank, was trying to single-handedly move the market. When a bank or trader is so powerful and deals in such numbers, they can often move the market with major trades. But sentiment was stronger after the earthquake and continued to keep the market down.

As time went by, it became harder and harder for the bank. They were holding massive positions which the whole market now knew about, and yet they were suppressed in an error account. Sooner or later, the market would either move back up to the bank's trading range and rescue them, or time would run out.

But soon the news was out, both in the local market and internationally. Barings had lost an amount possibly exceeding £800M, which was more than the bank's available capital. Barings Singapore activities had broken the entire bank.

In the City of London, all was gloom. It had always been expected that the Bank of England would step in to shore up a major banking institution that was going bust. But on this occasion, that decision was not made and the bank was allowed to go down. Institutions then rallied round with a view to buying the bank, which was soon sold to the ING Group.

The parallels with the Columbo scandal are illuminating. Once again, an alleged rogue trader - whether it be a branch of a bank or an individual trader, it doesn't matter - perhaps built up too great a belief in their own invincibility and began to take bigger and bigger positions.

Perhaps the resignation letter that Mr Leeson is alleged to have left on his desk says it all... "It was never my intention or aim for this to happen, but the pressures, both business and personal, have become too much to bear and have affected my health to the extent that a breakdown is imminent".

More Gamble than Proctor

People buying shares in Proctor and Gamble might have been forgiven for thinking that the core activity of the business they owned was that of providing washing up liquid and soap powder. To discover therefore that their business temporarily became derivatives trading, with catastrophic consequences, would be an unwelcome surprise.

In the 1980s and early 1990s, Proctor and Gamble, as an international trading organisation, had taken advantage of certain derivative contracts. It had been successful in the Swaps market, in matching its interest rate exposure and currency exposure to the particular assets or liabilities in question. However, in late 1993 and early 1994, the situation changed.

Proctor and Gamble wanted a $100 Million Swap contract on a fixed to floating basis. The point is that it considered rates would be falling, so it wanted to profit from the fact.

It approached a major bank who indicated that such a deal would be available, but that it would necessarily mean that if interest rates went up rather than down, Proctor and Gamble's returns would be greatly reduced. In order to change this, the contract was modified somewhat.

In November of 1993, a $200 Million contract was created as a five year Swap, on which there was an underlying option. If everything went Proctor and Gamble's way, they might have been paying interest at 75 points below their own commercial paper rate, for the entire period of the Swap. This would clearly be attractive as it would save some $7.5 Million over the period of the contract.

What Proctor and Gamble perhaps failed to understand was the risk to reward ratio. On the upside was a saving of $7.5 Million, and on the downside a figure at least 20 times that!

The problem was that for the contract, and a subsequent contract taken out some months later, to be able to work, the Swap rate had to remain within a narrow band. This is all very well if there was no interest rate volatility, but the effect of volatility was enormous.

The long and the short of it is that the way rates went, Proctor and Gamble would end up paying 1,400 basis points above their commercial paper rate, whilst the potential saving had only ever been 75 basis points. This gearing was clearly enormous, and Proctor and Gamble entered into serious discussions with their advisors as to whether or not they were made aware of the risk to reward ratio and whether any mitigating action could have been taken on the way to their losses, which were understood to have reached $157 Million.

Black Gold
Metallgesellschaft

Metallgesellschaft was one of Germany's largest and most respected companies. In the late 1980s it decided to diversify by buying an oil company. The merits of this as a commercial decision have, however, been somewhat obscured by the resulting derivative style catastrophe which took place.

Clearly, the management of Metallgesellschaft were concerned about oil prices. In an effort to buy market share, they guaranteed the price of heating oil for a decade, but gave customers the right to sell these contracts back to them if prices rose. This was most attractive for a customer.

In order to hedge against such a rise in oil prices, Metallgesellschaft took out Futures contracts. The problem it faced, however, is that Futures contracts were generally run for no more than a year, and so there was a gearing effect for a decade.

Of course, just like the dollar in the Columbo scandal, the Nikkei 225 in the Barings scandal, and interest rates in the Orange County scandal, the price of oil fell rather than rising as expected. Obviously, this led to considerable losses in the Futures market and margin calls.

As time went by, losses just accumulated, finally reaching $1.3 Billion, making this one of the most dramatic failures of a derivative hedging strategy ever recorded.

Have a nice day

Gibson Greetings in the United States produced greetings cards and wrapping paper. They began to consider derivatives as a means of hedging certain positions, and, like many others, perhaps moved into contracts that were not entirely appropriate, and which were not fully understood.

The management of Gibson Greetings felt that interest rates were on their way down. They bought derivative contracts which brought profits in the first year. However, after this intial success, matters took a turn for the worse. The result was that Gibson managed to lose over $20 Million - equivalent to an entire year of their profits and a significant percentage of their turnover.

Of course, in cases such as these, shareholders may have something of a complaint against the management. Were they authorised to deal in derivative contracts for any purpose other than hedging? When does hedging cease and trading begin? And what controls were in place to limit losses?

In the end, the company's advisors were given a $10 million civil penalty for violating reporting and anti-fraud provisions by giving Gibson Greetings 'innaccurate and understated' values of the loses it had suffered.

As time goes by, it is likely that more and more cases such as this will come to light. It is tempting for the management of a company, controlling purse strings in the tens of millions, to begin betting in order to improve the returns to investors. What seems to be a fundamental misunderstanding in all cases is that with a straight bet, you can lose only your stake money. With derivatives, you can lose your stake money and 100 times more!

Classic Over-Trading Syndrome

In the summer of 1999, Stephen Humphries was a young trader on the London International Financial Futures Exchange (LIFFE). His job was to trade in Gilt Futures (basically contracts written on Government Bonds). Like many before him he ran into difficulties and tried to "trade his way out". In fact, by the time he finished this exercise he had exceeded his own allowable trading limit by more than one hundred fold. His defence was basically that he had got "carried away". In fact, he ran up losses of £¾ million in less than two hours. That is £6,250 a minute! It is interesting to consider how far he would have got had he managed to somehow correct the position. Would he have gone on and on?

The owner of the company was forced to invest his own money in an attempt to keep the firm going, but in the end it went bust with losses of £2.3 million.

One of the most amazing aspects of this case is that Mr Humphries did not acknowledge that he had done anything wrong; He simply thought he had made a mistake.

Surely there is a common reason for concern in these stories. There is often a degree of self-delusion, where individuals and their managers seem to think that this is a game with few rules, which leads to these headline-making derivatives scandals. Properly enforced trading limits and a strong chain of command, with colleagues counter-signing deals, might well ensure less scandals occur.

Equitable Life

Equitable Life was the oldest mutual assurance company in the UK. Their story is unusual in that it demonstrates that things can go wrong if you don't use derivatives at all.

Insurance companies have traditionally sold pension plans to those who would retire many years into the future. And, to entice more customers, they have offered guaranteed annuity rates, which are effectively linked to interest rates. Of course, this tactic is fine in a time of sustained high interest rates, such as the 1970s, because individual pension holders would always choose the prevailing market rate over the guaranteed rate (which was usually somewhat smaller). However, over the following two decades, interest rates fell from double-digit returns to around 6%. What this meant, is that the guaranteed annuities were now highly attractive.

For example, an individual with a pension fund of £100,000 would get a pension of about £7,000 a year if he had no guarantee. Having a guarantee, such as those offered by Equitable Life, however, he would get as much as 14% a year, thus effectively doubling the value of his capital to him in terms of its income conversion qualities.

As interest rates fell, more and more policyholders decided to insist on their guaranteed annuity rates. At first, Equitable Life used all legal processes to try to avoid having to honour the guarantees they had made. However, in the High Court and then the House of Lords they were eventually defeated. At this point, they relied on other provisions within their policy documentation to avoid having to pay out the highest annuity rates. In the end, it became clear that their capital base simply could not sustain the guarantees that had been made. The organisation effectively put itself up for sale but there were no buyers (initially at least). Eventually they became a closed fund accepting no further new business and the policyholders were all left with punitive penalties should they wish to take their money and run.

Of course, by participating in long-term interest rate contracts, the Equitable Life could have hedged its exposure. However, they had effectively written a one-way long-term interest rate option, and with the rapidly increasing value of their fund, this clearly went out of control. This is a case, therefore, where knowledge of derivatives and hedging techniques could have saved the company.

Summary

There have been a great many other less well-known scandals, and probably some that have not been reported. These are problems of concern to anyone with a mortgage or even a pension policy. Most innocent investors will have no idea whether the managers of their mutual funds or their pension funds are taking unsustainable positions based in derivatives.

But it is not the derivative instruments themselves that are to blame, any more than motor manufacturers are to blame for road accidents, or fire-arms manufacturers for war. It is the use of these instruments by the individuals and corporations who trade them, which seem to be at fault. The following factors would appear to be common to most scandals.

1. A period of successful trading, probably just hedging or writing simpler contracts.

2. A move into more complex areas, with greater gearing and more danger.

3. Unsupervised individuals taking large positions based on their own judgement and expectations.

4. Those same individuals, still unsupervised, increasing their positions still further to try to compensate for markets going the wrong way.

5. Losses coming to light, and trading ceasing.

Meltdown!

Finally, let's imagine the case of the 'super' rogue trader. Slowly but surely, he builds himself up as the most successful trader in world financial markets. The corporation he works for becomes sufficiently profitable to buy out other players in the top 10. Before long, he is chief trader in the world's biggest financial institution and controlling half the market's wealth.

Imagine that half the wealth in the world is invested in world stock markets, and there is a crash whereby they halve in value. At this stage our rogue trader places a massive bet. He writes a Call option on the whole market in every different financial centre, receiving a massive premium for doing so. But the market bounces back to its original level and he has now lost one half of the value of the world's stock markets, or a quarter of the entire wealth in the world. On sentiment, the rest of the wealth in the world then permeates into the stock market, doubling it again in value. The rogue trader has now lost three quarters of all the money in the world, and as he doesn't have it, there must necessarily be a collapse of the trading system.

It may sound far fetched, but in the last five years alone, tens of billions of pounds have been reported lost in the many scandals, some of which are discussed above. Whilst *the entire derivatives market may well be worth some seven and a half trillion pounds*, this is little comfort - imagine the gearing on that, and how that might go wrong!

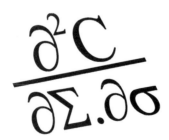

$$\frac{\partial^2 C}{\partial \Sigma . \partial \sigma}$$

Chapter 9

The Psychology of Trading

Before you consider trading in the markets, you will need to have worked out your attitude to certain crucial research issues, and a system which best suits your own psychology.

Research Systems

There are two schools of thought in derivatives markets. The first is fundamental analysis and the second is technical analysis.

Fundamental Analysis

This involves collecting and studying economic data relating to supply and demand in order to forecast likely future price movements. You have to take into account every possible contingency. You must understand economics, trends and so-on in great depth. This should, of course, be relatively simple in theory. You would look at a year's production in a particular commodity, and any overhang from last year. This should give you the ability to predict demand.

However, you need to be aware of other factors. For example, one trader may have a disproportionate or disguised position. Further, there could be a major political or economic development which affects the position such as, the recent Northern Europe BSE epidemic that had huge effects on the price of beef.

Fundamental analysis is clearly an important method in giving yourself an edge in producing your forecasts. But you do have to be aware that the position can change rapidly as a result of some unforeseen factor.

Technical Analysis

This is perhaps far more interesting to the derivatives trader. There are a great many critics of technical analysis because of how it works. It seeks to express past price movements as part of a trend, and then simply assumes they will carry on in the future. So if the price of gold has been increasing at a steady rate over the previous six months, the technical analyst might look at this, draw a line on a chart, and then continue that line showing further growth for the subsequent six months.

At this point many people abandon technical analysis. How can a simple drawing of a line on a piece of paper seek to express the change in price of an asset so closely bound up with the intricacies and complexities of the world economy? Of course it can't. But what it can do, however, is make the market aware that this is what a vast number of participants think. They will believe that gold is continuing to rise, and will therefore buy it. This means that those who don't believe in technical analysis will also have to buy it, and lo and behold, price continues to increase.

But there is much more to it than that. Imagine for example that the trading range of a particular stock or commodity can be expressed between two parallel lines on a graph. At some stage, the line of the price chart may "break out" or pull back from one of these trend lines, either at the top or the bottom. When this happens it will be a selling or buying signal for many, even those who do not believe in technical analysis as discussed above.

Perhaps an individual simply said to himself, "when gold reaches $400 an ounce I am out". Perhaps he has placed a trailing stop or a limit order. However, there could be something much more fundamental about it. When gold reaches a certain price for example, it is a hedge against inflation.

Further, when inflation reaches a certain level, gold is still a hedge against inflation! When stock markets or other intangibles start to crash, there is a flight to quality, which includes the reality of holding a precious metal. So the whole thing is interrelated. But nonetheless, the chartists sit back with their mechanical programmes and carry a disciplined way forward.

Other Factors

Of course, there are a great many other factors. Some analysts believe in the laws of nature and that certain trends are repeated as cycles. There is peak demand for a certain commodity at a certain time of year. And there may be other cycles that are shorter or longer than the seasons themselves.

Elliott waves are based on the principle that market behaviour ebbs and flows in recognisable patterns and that these patterns are repeated.

Many believe in Gann numbers, and that precise mathematical patterns govern everything in the universe.

The point is, that you need to be aware of all these different factors before you finally decide what your own view is. Moreover, once you have decided what you believe, you will need still to be aware of what other people believe because it will have a direct bearing on your overall results.

For more information on technical analysis, including waves and cycles, may I refer you to *Timing the Financial Markets* by Alex Kiam, also published by TTL.

Psychology

Imagine you have to decorate your living room. One of the walls has a window right in the middle. Some people will approach the task by carefully painting around the window aperture and around all the edges of the wall before finally going through to fill in the large spaces. Others would choose to fill in all the large spaces first and then go round the edges. It is all a question of psychology. Are you the sort of person who wants to see an *immediate* improvement, in which case you will paint as much of the wall you can before the time consuming detail work, or are you somebody who is patient and happy to build up to the grand finale of filling in the large spaces?

You must try to analyse your personality from this perspective, and see whether you are a conceptual person or a detail person, and then plan your trading strategy accordingly.

If you follow trends or concepts, you might consider that an ageing population will lead to a demand for a particular commodity and decide therefore to follow that trend across that commodity or stock and all its derivatives.

Alternatively, you could be much more focused on detail. You might consider for example that oil is a currency in itself, and a great deal is known about it and you could then concentrate purely on short-term oil contracts. You would become extremely expert in a narrow field. You simply have to decide which type of trading is likely to be most suitable for you.

The Psychology of Losing

What breaks many traders is the fact of continual losses in derivative contracts. The vast majority of contracts simply expire worthless. Even the best traders lose money up to 49% of the time. You have to be able to stand this and you have to able to judge a losing period by the timescales you have set. For example, some traders have to be ahead at the end of every single day. Others take a fortnightly view. For others, it can be as much as six months.

If you are a daily trader, then you will be looking to take very short-term positions and you will need to get results immediately. You certainly could not look to a six month trend in your results or you would soon be out of business! However, if you are taking longer positions, then you will need to be a more relaxed person who is not so keen to see immediate results.

More significantly, whatever strategy you take, you will need to be able to stand losses. You will be wrong for a very large proportion of the time and you will need to be able to accept that without moving outside your set limits or panicking.

There are so many traders who have gone out of business, where if they had simply stuck to their original aims, stayed within their limits, and gritted their teeth, would have traded out of a downturn in their cycle. If you talk to the longest-lived, most successful traders, they will all tell you that to keep faith with your system, to close out losing positions quickly, and to let your profits run to predetermined points, is absolutely fundamental.

Risk Banding

No one should trade derivatives as their only investment activity. Even the most successful traders constantly pull profits out of their portfolios and place them in more reliable, if less lucrative financial instruments.

Even in my own case, the amount I have traded in derivatives is only a fraction of my total wealth. The point is, that you might well lose your entire stake in derivative transactions, and if you trade the wrong way, (i.e. short in the market), then you could eat in to the rest of your wealth.

It makes sense therefore to employ "risk banding". With this method you would effectively construct a pyramid of investment. The lower risk investments would all be at the base of the pyramid to give it a solid foundation. So you might have cash, national savings certificates, treasury bonds and the like, giving you a solid base. Above that you might have with-profit funds or lower risk mutual funds. The next level up would be higher risk mutual funds, perhaps in overseas markets. The next band would be individual equities and the top band would include derivative instruments.

If you are relatively risk-averse overall, then your pyramid will be low and wide. However, if you are more of a high risk investor, then you would have a tall narrow pyramid, where the base of lower investments was not such a high proportion, and where the peak could be as much as 25% of your overall wealth.

You need to decide how to band your investments, so that when trading in derivatives markets, you are not constrained by feeling that you are a low or medium risk investor, because you have already taken care of that aspect of your affairs through the lower levels of your risk pyramid.

The Golden Rules of Trading

It should be understood that option trading is not for everybody. Those who will be successful are likely to be a very small number of those who begin trading. In the professional market, the players are split between those who have an incredible calm equanimity and manage to remain still as a mill pond despite all the frenetic activity around them. The others are on the fast track to burnout, living on their nerves and suffering overtly from stress.

As a private investor, you will need to be in the former category to ensure that your decisions are not made emotionally, or irrationally. If you stick to the following golden rules, you should reduce the risk of failure:

1.   **DON'T GO NAKED** - As a private investor you should not be writing uncovered positions.

2.   **CREATE YOUR PLAN AND STICK TO IT** - Before you begin trading, create a game plan detailing the amount you will have at risk at any one time, the type of contracts in which you will be involved, and what you will do if prices move outside a set trading range. You must then stick to this plan in order to limit losses and to protect gains.

3.   **TAKE YOUR PROFITS, CLOSE YOUR POSITIONS** - If you have set a particular level for a profit and it arises, take it. Waiting for more simply means that you will be confused as to whether you should take it. If that profit then is lost, you will be tempted to move outside other limits you have to try to regain it.

4.   **NEVER BE INVINCIBLE** - Always be modest and never believe in your own infallibility; this will lead you to take sensible positions and close them out according to your plan.

Chapter Ten

In Conclusion

By now you will have a very clear idea of the various different derivative markets and how they operate. If you are intending to trade yourself, then the easiest and simplest method would be to open a traded options account with a stockbroker.

Because of the bad press which derivatives have received, and because of the dangers of trading, you might find this difficult and would perhaps need to establish your credentials before a major broker would want to take you on. Additionally, you might be required to deposit the stock if you are writing short positions or Call options.

Like any relationship, you will need to be honest from the outset and build up a rapport with your broker. In the first instance, you may find yourself having very long conversations as you feel your way in the market. This means that the broker talking to you will probably be losing money.

As time goes by, however, you should be able to make your trades and orders very quickly, and probably deal with increased confidence and regularity. The Stock Exchange will provide a list of stockbrokers to whom you might apply to open an account, and it might be useful to consider one of the regional groups so that you could visit the office and build up a rapport if necessary.

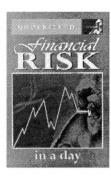

Understand Financial Risk in a Day

Risk management is all about minimising risks and maximising opportunities. Those who understand what they should be doing, as a result of their risk calculations, will usually come out as winners. Those who flail in the dark will, more often than not, be the losers.

Understand Financial Risk in a Day is a perfect introduction to the subject. Light on detailed formulae and heavy on easy-to-follow examples it will lead the reader to a greater awareness of how to evaluate the risks they are facing and adapt a strategy to create the best possible outcome.

96 Pages   *ISBN: 1-873668-24-4*   *£6.95*

Understand Swaps in a Day

Swaps and Swap bi-products are being used by all financial institutions, major quoted companies and governments around the world. This book offers a practical introduction to the subject for those with little or no knowledge of the Swap markets. Learn:

- How Swaps have transformed financial markets
- What they are and how they work in simple terms
- Interest rate, currency and esoteric swap structures
- Importance of swaps to traders and treasurers
- Also, swap valuations, accounting, tax, capital adequacy and othér aspects.

128 Pages   *ISBN: 1-873668-74-0*   *£6.95*

Timing the Financial Markets

Charting your way to profits. Shows all levels of investors how to construct charts and graphs of price movements for bonds, shares and commodities. Then it explains, in easy-to-understand language, how to interpret the results and turn them into profit. With computers taking over so much of the trading activity on the world's stockmarkets (news programmes call it "automated trading"), charting is becoming a more and more powerful technique.

96 Pages   *ISBN: 1-873668-47-3*   *£6.95*

Investing in Traded Options

In jargon-free, easy-to-follow language, Investing in Traded Options takes all the mystery out of the options market. It successfully bridges the gap between the mundane experience of buying and selling shares and the exciting world of traded options.

You'll find simple examples, with accompanying diagrams, which will enable you to calculate and control the risks you are taking. By the end, you will have all the information you need to make informed decisions about the way you can use options trading to make extra profit or protect existing gains.

160 Pages (hardback)   ISBN: 1-873668-24-4   £14.95

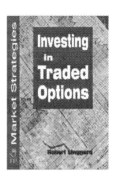

NLP for Traders and Investors

Neuro-Linguistic Programming (NLP) gives you the power to understand the critical psychology that sorts winners from losers in the markets and achieve lasting change in your life. ✔ What makes people tick - especially under pressure? ✔ How to understand the psychology of market players, which no computer can copy ✔ How to model the strategies of winners - you've read what they say, now get inside their minds and do as they do! ✔ Personal strategies to give you the edge over those using just fundamental and technical analysis.

160 Pages   ISBN: 1-873668-481-3   £12.95

International Dictionary of Derivatives

A dictionary of terms designed to aid all those involved, or about to become involved, with these complex financial instruments. Nothing is missed out, with explanations and diagrams from Accrual Options and Agrigation through to ZEPOs and Zero Gain Collars. Also contains an extensive list of acronyms.

96 Pages   ISBN: 1-873668-57-0   £6.95

Book Ordering

Please complete the form below or use a plain piece of paper and send it to the address given. You may also order online at www.takethat.co.uk.

Europe/Asia
TTL, PO Box 200, Harrogate, North Yorks HG1 2YR, England
(or fax to 01423-526035, or email: sales@net-works.co.uk).

USA/Canada
Trafalgar Square, PO Box 257, Howe Hill Road, North Pomfret, Vermont 05053 (or fax to 802-457-1913, call toll free 800-423-4525, or email: tsquare@sover.net)

Postage and handling charge:
UK - £1 for first book, and 50p for each additional book
USA - $5 for first book, and $2 for each additional book (all shipments by UPS, please provide street address).
Elsewhere - £3 for first book, and £1.50 for each additional book via surface post (for airmail and courier rates, please fax or email for a price quote)

Book	Qty	Price
	Postage	
☐ I enclose payment for £_____	**Total:**	
☐ Please debit my Visa/Amex/Mastercard		

No: ☐☐☐☐ - ☐☐☐☐ - ☐☐☐☐ - ☐☐☐☐

Expiry Date: ☐☐☐☐   Signature: _____

Name:Mr/Mrs/Miss: _____

Address: _____

_____

_____

Postcode/Zip: _____ Country:_____

derivbk3